Strange
New Land

AFRICANS IN
COLONIAL AMERICA

Strange
New Land

AFRICANS IN

COLONIAL AMERICA

Peter H. Wood

OXFORD
UNIVERSITY PRESS

OXFORD
UNIVERSITY PRESS

Oxford   New York
Auckland   Bangkok   Buenos Aires   Cape Town   Chennai
Dar es Salaam   Delhi   Hong Kong   Istanbul   Karachi   Kolkata
Kuala Lumpur   Madrid   Melbourne   Mexico City   Mumbai   Nairobi
São Paulo   Shanghai   Singapore   Taipei   Tokyo   Toronto

Copyright © 1996, 2003 by Peter H. Wood

Published by Oxford University Press, Inc.
198 Madison Avenue, New York, New York 10016
http://www.oup-usa.org

Library of Congress Cataloging-in-Publication Data is
available upon request.

9 8 7 6 5 4 3 2 1

Printed in the United States of America on acid-free paper

Design: Megan Rickards Youngquist

Frontispiece: *Inspection and sale of a negro,* by Whitney,
Jocelyn & Annin, 1854

For Lil,
with love

Contents

Strange
New Land

AFRICANS IN

COLONIAL AMERICA

Buried Beyond
the Fence

MORE THAN TWO HUNDRED fifty years ago, New York City built a fence. The colonial settlement lacked protection against French and Indian raiders coming down the Hudson River from the north, so in 1745 black and white inhabitants were put to work constructing a log wall that stretched all the way from the Hudson to the East River. South of this crude boundary, on the tip of Manhattan Island, stood the expanding town that a century earlier had been the Dutch village of New Amsterdam. The new fortification, built along what is now Chambers Street, guarded the homes, gardens, and churchyards of the thriving township; it even sheltered the local jail.

The low wetland to the north, just outside the wooden palisade, contained plots that the authorities preferred to exclude from the community. There stood the town's powder house, surrounded by a pond of fresh water to limit the danger if the gunpowder exploded. And there stood a graveyard assigned to African Americans. It appears clearly on a 1755 map, labeled "Negros Burial Ground."

The location of this graveyard beyond the fence was not accidental. In 1697, the city had passed a law excluding blacks from white churchyards in lower Manhattan, and the African population, already more than 700 people, had taken over a desolate site well beyond the town limits. During the 18th century, the field just east of Broadway became the resting place for well over 10,000 persons. A few were European strangers and poor whites, but most were black New Yorkers, both slave and free. In 1745, when the fence was built, more than twenty percent of all New York residents were black, and life expectancy was short. So funerals were frequent and the burial ground filled up rapidly. By the time of the American Revolution, new caskets were being stacked above the old, and after 1790 other graveyards were established as the city expanded. By the late twentieth century, the cemetery, located two blocks north of New York's City Hall, had been covered over by a parking lot and forgotten.

Then suddenly, in 1990, New York City sold the parking lot between Duane and Reade Streets for the construction of a new government office building, and the black burial ground was rediscovered. Since lower Manhattan is one of the world's busiest places, much had been destroyed by generations of builders. But several spots directly under the city streets had never been disturbed. By 1992, archaeologists had excavated the remains of some 420 individuals—men, women, and children. It had been two centuries since the plot had closed, and the people buried there had lacked many worldly possessions. And yet, in coffins resting sixteen to twenty-eight feet below street level, specialists could still find revealing clues. A man had been killed by a musket ball; a woman had been buried with glass beadwork and symbolic African cowrie shells. According to city archaeologist Dan Pagano, "It's like finding lost volumes of African-American history."

After resting silently for more than 200 years, these fragile remains were swiftly surrounded by a swirl of national publicity and controversy. A scientific team from Howard University received permission to transport the bones to their laboratory, so they could be analyzed carefully and then respectfully returned to the ground. Meanwhile, after much public debate, the site itself appears destined to be preserved. Black musician Noel Pointer teamed with local groups to collect more than 100,000 signatures on a petition seeking landmark status for the burial ground. As Pointer put it, "The bones of our ancestors have risen again to remind us of the pain and promise that is the African-American journey in America."

This book is about the pain and promise of the black heritage in colonial America. For too long the story of African arrival and survival in this strange new land has remained buried and nearly forgotten outside the fence of conventional American history. Recently, historians and archaeologists have made dramatic headway in unearthing the general outlines and rich details of this complicated and powerful story. They are rediscovering, first of all, what a long story it is. Early black history in North America begins shortly after the arrival of Columbus in the New World, and it stretches out from the time of Esteban, the sixteenth-century explorer of the Southwest, to the days of Crispus Attucks, the eighteenth-century sailor who died in the Boston Massacre. This initial journey covers two and a half centuries—more time than all the dramatic chapters of African-American history from the American Revolution to the present day.

Scholars are also rediscovering what a varied story lies hidden in this distant period. The lives of our earliest African-American ancestors were as diverse as the graves in which they were eventually laid to rest—and we can still see how different those gravesites were. When you visit an isolated slave cemetery in the Georgia Sea Islands, you can encounter traditions brought from the Kongo-Angola region of Africa, where graves were decorated with the last-used or most-favored objects of the deceased. Cups and pitchers are broken to release their power and turned upside down to assist the traveler in the next world; shining objects are polished so the sun's rays can reflect the continuing "flash" of the departed spirit.

In contrast, when you visit colonial cemeteries in New England, you can confront very different memorials. In the corner of a country churchyard in Jaffrey, New Hampshire, I have seen the headstone of Violate, a black woman born in 1729. She and her daughter were the slaves of James Baldwin of Woburn, Massachusetts, and they were purchased and freed by an African-born leather tanner named Amos Fortune, who had bought his own liberty in 1769. Violate was fifty when she married him, and, according to her large slate gravestone, she was seventy-three when she died, having outlived her husband by less than a year. They are buried side by side, beneath matching headstones, and the inscriptions are still legible after 200 years:

<table>
<tr><td>Sacred</td><td>Sacred</td></tr>
<tr><td>to the memory of</td><td>to the memory of</td></tr>
<tr><td>Amos Fortune</td><td>Violate</td></tr>
<tr><td>who was born free in</td><td>by sale the slave of</td></tr>
<tr><td>Africa a slave in America</td><td>Amos Fortune by</td></tr>
<tr><td>he purchased liberty</td><td>marriage his wife by</td></tr>
<tr><td>professed Christianity</td><td>her fidelity his friend</td></tr>
<tr><td>lived reputably and</td><td>and solace she died</td></tr>
<tr><td>died hopefully</td><td>his widow</td></tr>
<tr><td>Nov. 17, 1801</td><td>Sept. 13, 1802</td></tr>
<tr><td>Aet. 91</td><td>Aet. 91</td></tr>
</table>

Also legible, just barely, is a very different marker in God's Acre, the Moravian graveyard in Old Salem, North Carolina. The small rectangular stone, laid flat in the ground amid row upon row of similar markers, seems to say "ABRA'AM NEGER Guinea" (meaning that Abraham the Negro was born in Africa), and the faint numbers suggest that he died in 1797 at the age of 67. It was shown to me recently by my friend Jon Sensbach, who has researched the life of Abraham and the other black slaves in the records of the Moravian community. "Our dear Brother Abraham . . . , a Negro from the Mandingo Nation on the coast of African Guinea, was born about the year 1730," states a brief account preserved in the church archives. Captured in war as a young man and sold into slavery, he had been brought in 1771 to Salem, where he married and joined the church. Like Amos Fortune, he worked as a leather tanner until his death. Following Moravian tradition, he was buried beside the other married brethren of the community—and only a few feet away from the man who had been his master.

For each marked grave, such as Abraham's, there are hundreds, even thousands, of unmarked graves like those placed outside the palisade in eighteenth-century New York. We can never bring back these African-American forebears from the colonial past, but we can work to remove at last the fences that have separated and hidden them for so long. In a sense, their weary bones and their proud spirits rest under all the huge buildings in the strange new land called America. This is a portion of their story.

CHAPTER 1

The Earliest Africans in North America

IN THE SUMMER OF 1619, a 160-ton ship from the port of Flushing in Holland sailed into Chesapeake Bay. This Dutch vessel was under the command of Captain Jope and piloted by an Englishman named Marmaduke Raynor. They were seeking to obtain provisions after a season of raiding in the West Indies. In exchange for supplies, Jope and his crew sold more than twenty Negroes to the local authorities in the struggling English colony of Virginia. These black newcomers came ashore twelve years after the founding of Jamestown and one year before the *Mayflower* arrived at Plymouth in New England. The people brought to Virginia by the Dutch man-of-war are often cited as the first persons of African ancestry to set foot on North America. But in fact, others had come before them and had traveled widely through the southern part of the continent.

The earliest Africans to reach North America arrived nearly 500 years ago as participants in the large expeditions organized by Spanish-speaking explorers. These Spaniards were the successors to Christopher Columbus, and in the generation after

1492 they fanned out across the Caribbean, competing to find a passage to the Orient and to locate gold and other riches. They exploited the local inhabitants ruthlessly as they advanced. Within several decades, constant warfare, strange diseases, and brutal enslavement had destroyed the native population of the West Indies. The Spanish colonizers immediately began searching for new supplies of labor.

One solution to the labor shortage was the transportation of additional workers from Europe, but most of these people were practicing Christians, so fellow Christians felt reluctant to exploit them. The Catholic church in Rome and the Spanish government in Seville had less concern about exploiting non-Christian Indians, so a second option centered upon Native Americans. Expeditions were sent out from the Caribbean in various directions to the American mainland, seeking inhabitants who could be enslaved. But this strategy also presented problems. Some groups resisted fiercely, and others died rapidly from diseases the Europeans had unknowingly carried with them from across the Atlantic. The aggressive Spanish empire-builders wanted more slaves than they could get in the Americas. Thus they began to seek more distant sources of labor, and soon they focused upon a third Atlantic region: the West Coast of Africa.

By 1500, European ships had been trading along the coast of West Africa for several generations. Besides purchasing gold and ivory, they also bought slaves and transported them north for sale in Europe. Soon the Spanish began diverting some of these slave-trading vessels to the Caribbean. Many of the first African workers found themselves forced to clear land for plantations or to dig for gold and silver. But others were pressed into service as soldiers, sailors, and servants. They were present, therefore, when the Spanish conquistador Hernán Cortés marched against the Aztecs in Mexico in 1519 and when Francisco Pizarro attacked the Incas in Peru twelve years later.

Africans were also present in the early Spanish forays onto the continent of North America, as Juan Ponce de León and his successors probed Florida and the Gulf Coast in search of slaves, wealth, and a passage to the Pacific. In August 1526, for example, six Spanish ships landed on the coast of what is now South Carolina. Their commander, Lucas Vásquez de Ayllón, brought at least 500 people—men, women, and children— along with 100 horses and enough cattle, sheep, and pigs to start a settlement. They pushed south along the coast to find a suitable location, and they constructed a small village of thatched-roof huts. But within months Ayllón died, and bitter tensions arose over who should succeed him. In the midst of this struggle for control, African slaves set fire to some of the houses at night. Divided and embittered, 150 survivors straggled back to the Caribbean as winter set in. Almost all the rest—more than 350 people—died because of sickness, violence, hunger, or cold. But it was rumored that some of the Africans had escaped their bondage and remained to live among the coastal Indians.

That same winter the Spanish king approved another expedition to the Florida region, and five ships, commanded by Pánfilo de Narváez, set sail from Spain in June 1527. The following spring more than 400 soldiers and servants, including some men of African descent, landed near Tampa Bay and marched northwest. They hoped to make great conquests, but they were poorly prepared and badly led. The Indians fought fiercely to defend their own lands, and soon the invaders were separated from their supply boats and from each other. Most died in the Gulf Coast wilderness, but a few survived long enough to be taken in by local tribes. Miraculously, four such men encountered one another on the Texas coast in 1534. They evaded the tribes with whom they were living and set off across the Southwest in hopes of reaching Mexico City, the capital of the Spanish colony of New Spain.

One of these four survivors was a Spanish-speaking African named Esteban (Stephen)—the first African to emerge clearly in the pages of North American history. Another survivor was a Spanish officer named Álvar Núñez Cabeza de Vaca who wrote down their incredible story. He told how they had been enslaved by Indians and forced to haul wood and water, living on nuts, rabbits, spiders, and the juice of prickly pears. Heading west, they viewed the rolling Texas prairie with its herds of buffalo. "Over all the region," they reported, "we saw vast and beautiful plains that would make good pasture." They also marveled at the variety of languages they encountered among Southwestern Indians. Cabeza de Vaca noted that "there are a thousand dialectical differences," adding that Esteban served as their primary go-between. "He was constantly in conversation, finding out about routes, towns, and other matters we wished to know."

After eight years in America, including two years traveling together through the Southwest, the four men finally reached Mexico City in 1536—the first newcomers from Europe and Africa to cross the huge expanse of North America. When they described the massive Indian apartment dwellings they had seen (known as pueblos), gold-hungry listeners assumed they had glimpsed the legendary and wealthy Seven Cities of Cíbola. Soon Governor Antonio de Mendoza, the first Spanish viceroy of Mexico, organized a new exploration to seek out these seven mythical towns, which were supposedly surrounded by turquoise-studded walls of gold. Since the black man was a skilled translator and a seasoned guide who remained enslaved, Mendoza purchased Esteban and presented him to a Spanish friar named Marcos de Niza, who had been selected to lead the expedition. In March 1539, the friar's party, "with the Negro and other slaves, and Indians," headed northward toward what is now Arizona in search of Cíbola. According to an official report:

> The Lord Viceroy having . . . news and notice of such land sent a friar and a negro, the latter having come from Florida with the others . . . as survivors of the party taken there by Pánfilo Narváez. These set out with the knowledge the negro had in order to go to a very rich country, as the latter declared, and told the friar . . . that there are seven very populous cities with great buildings. . . . They have houses built of stone and lime, being of three stories, and with great quantities of turquoises set in doors and windows.

Esteban, familiar with the region, proceeded ahead with his two dogs and a number of Indians. As the summer heat increased, he sent wooden crosses back to the Christian friar to assure him of their progress. Finally he approached a large community—probably the pueblo of Zuni in western New Mexico. Hoping to have reached "Cíbola" at last, Esteban sent messengers ahead as usual, carrying "his great Mace made of a gourd," which "had a string of belles upon it, and two feathers one white and another red, in token that he demanded safe conduct, and that he came peaceably." But the Zunis quickly recognized the bells as Spanish. They linked this party advancing from the south with rumors of Spanish slave raiding and violence that were already circulating in the Indian markets of the region. Zuni leaders blamed the appearance of foreigners for deaths that had already occurred, and they feared a plot by which "neither man nor woman of them shall remaine unslaine."

When Esteban's messengers returned, they reported handing over the "great gourd" to the Indian magistrate. He "tooke the same in his hands, and after he had spyed the belles, in a great rage and fury hee cast it to the ground, and willed the messengers to get them packing with speed, for he knew well ynough what people they were, and that they should . . . in no case enter the citie, for if they did hee would put them all to death." Determined in his course and confident that diplomacy could prevail, Esteban dismissed this initial rejection as "no great matter" and proceeded to approach the town. But armed men blocked his entrance to the city and confined him to an outlying building. They denied him food and water overnight, and they confiscated his trade goods. Negotiations proved unsuccessful, and when Esteban emerged the next morning, he and most of his company were attacked and killed by an angry crowd. Though "bloody and wounded in many places," several of his Indian companions managed to survive. They returned southward to inform Fray Marcos of the death of his experienced black guide.

The failure of the expeditions of Ayllón, Narváez, and Fray Marcos only increased the ambitions of other explorers. Their ventures into the American interior would also include the presence of Africans at every stage. Even before the death of Esteban at the Zuni pueblo, other black Hispanic soldiers and slaves were among those preparing to accompany Francisco Vázquez de Coronado into the Southwest and Hernando de Soto into the Southeast, and a few remain visible in the surviving accounts. Among those marching with de Soto, for example, was a man named "Gomez, a negro belonging to Vasco

Gonçalez who spoke good Spanish." In 1537, de Soto had received permission to invade Florida and carve out a province for himself and his followers in the southern interior. The Spanish crown had authorized him to raise an army, to establish three fortified towns, and to include as many as 50 enslaved Negroes in his plans. Gomez was among the black men forced to take part in this ambitious design.

When the expedition landed in Florida in May 1539, it contained 330 foot soldiers and almost as many others—artisans, carpenters, cooks, servants, and priests. They also brought herds of hogs and other livestock that would accompany their army to provide fresh meat. De Soto had taken part in Pizarro's successful campaign against the golden cities of the Incas in Peru. Now he was anxious to discover an equally wealthy kingdom of his own. But long marches through the swamps and forests of the Deep South revealed no such prize, even when he tortured local leaders for information and pushed his own company to extremes. The more de Soto's ambition was frustrated, the more ruthless his invasion became. At the Indian town of Cofitachequi near the Savannah River, he finally received gifts of pearls in the spring of 1540. But he thanked the young woman leader (or *cacica*) who had presented the pearls by making her a captive in her own region and obliging her to march with his soldiers to assure their safe passage in her domain.

De Soto's repeated cruelty toward the Native Americans assured that few would give him a kindly reception. His ruthlessness with his own army meant that many were willing to risk desertion in a strange land, especially slaves who stood to gain nothing from the entire enterprise. Several weeks after de Soto's departure from Cofitachequi, his royal Indian prisoner stepped off the path with several servants and made good her escape.

Several members of de Soto's company also disappeared, including three Spanish-speaking slaves: an Indian boy from Cuba, a Berber from North Africa, and a West African—Gomez. The first two slaves eventually returned to camp and begged forgiveness, reporting that Gomez had elected to remain behind with the young Indian. Regarding the black man and the Native American woman, these informants said, "it was very certain that they held communication as husband and wife, and that both had made up their minds" to go to Cofitachequi.

So by 1540, less than fifty years after the arrival of Columbus in the Caribbean, an African ex-slave and an Indian *cacica* were living together in the southern forest. By now other European countries, jealous of Spanish wealth in the New World, were beginning to show an interest in the coast of North America. Several explorers sailing for the French king envisioned the possibility of discovering a short "Northwest Passage" from the Atlantic to the Pacific. Giovanni da Verrazzano hoped to find a route to the Orient when he examined the Outer Banks of Carolina and the mouth of New York harbor in 1524. Jacques Cartier had similar ambitions when he sailed up the broad St. Lawrence River in 1535. Even if they could not discover access to the Pacific, Spain's rivals could take advantage of the excellent fishing grounds in the North Atlantic. Or, if they dared, they could go after grander targets, attacking the Spanish galleons that sailed homeward regularly from Mexico.

The annual Spanish fleet, carrying gold and silver from the New World to Seville, followed the currents of the Gulf Stream northward along the Florida Peninsula. Foreign ships, lying in wait along that coastline, could easily attack and capture stray vessels before they headed across the Atlantic. In 1565, therefore, the Spanish established a garrison at St. Augustine on the east coast of Florida. The purpose of this small port town was to help protect the passing gold fleet from marauders and to secure Spain's claim to the Florida region against European rivals. It became the first permanent non-Indian settlement in North America, and Africans were present there from the beginning.

By 1600, roughly forty Africans had been transported to the small outpost of St. Augustine as property of the royal garrison; another sixty had arrived in the households of private individuals. These early African Americans—mostly men and mostly Spanish-speaking—were involved in erecting more than 100 Spanish-owned shops and houses and in building Fort San Marcos on the northern edge of town. They planted gardens and fished in the Matanzas River, selling their catch in the local fish market. Those who had accepted Christianity worshipped at the local Catholic church, and some drew token pay for themselves and their owners as drummers, fifers, and flag bearers in the local militia.

But living conditions were harsh, and controls at the remote outpost were limited. So some Africans escaped to live among the Indians, as Gomez and others had done several generations earlier. A Spanish document from 1605 complained that slaves had slipped away toward the south and intermarried with the Ais tribe living along the Florida coast. Those who remained in town had little reason for allegiance to their owners. The authorities feared that they would support any invader who offered them their freedom, and one official, writing in 1606, warned others to be wary of "persons of their kind, who are the worst enemies we can have." More than a century later St. Augustine would be viewed as a potential haven by a later generation of black Southerners, but that day was still far in the future.

Just as blacks, both enslaved and free, took part in the exploration and colonization of Spanish Florida, they also participated
in the creation of a new colony in the Southwest. There, from
the time of Esteban, Spanish raiding parties had carried Indian
captives back to Mexico to work in the silver mines alongside
enslaved Africans. Before the end of the sixteenth century,
Mexican adventurers pushed to gain control of the populated
region along the upper Rio Grande. Their reasons for immi-
grating to this region were many and varied: Some hoped to
limit the exploitation of local Indians; some hoped to convert
the Indians to Christianity; some hoped to control them and
extract a profit. Government officials hoped to prevent
European rivals from discovering wealth that had so far eluded
the Spanish. But most of the settlers simply hoped to escape
harsh conditions in *old* Mexico and take their chances on the
rough frontier in a colony to be called *New* Mexico.

In 1595, a contract for this northern venture was awarded to
Don Juan de Oñate, one of the last in a long line of ambitious
and violent conquistadors stretching back to Cortés and
Pizarro, de Soto and Coronado. Oñate put up the enormous
wealth his father had gained from silver mining (largely with
Indian and African labor) in exchange for the right to conquer,
control, and exploit a vast region. His tactics proved strikingly
ruthless, even in an era known for its brutality, and his grandest
ambitions were never realized. In 1599 he crushed a desperate
Indian revolt at the pueblo of Acoma so ferociously that he was
reprimanded for his acts, and eventually he was forced to with-
draw from his newly founded colony. By 1608 there was serious
talk of abandoning the settlement of New Mexico altogether.
Nevertheless, by 1610 a permanent mission had been established
at Santa Fe, and many of those who had accompanied

Oñate had demonstrated their determination to remain in New Mexico.

In 1598, the first contingent of 500 colonists heading north included persons of varied racial backgrounds and social ranks. These newcomers to the Southwest included black and mulatto (that is, mixed-race) men and women, both enslaved and free. For example, three enslaved Negro women and a variety of mulatto servants, both male and female, accompanied one wealthy Spanish settler, and other households were undoubtedly similar. Authorities in Mexico, anxious to prevent runaways from escaping to another province, ordered the death penalty for any Indian or mulatto attempting to migrate without presenting clear identification. So when several hundred reinforcements headed north in 1600, nonwhites had to obtain clearance to depart. One mulatto, branded on the face as a slave, showed that his owner had given him permission to take part in the journey. Twenty-year-old Mateo Montero, another mulatto with a slave brand on his face, proved that the master who had purchased him twelve years earlier had recently granted him freedom. Isabel, a free mulatto woman traveling alone, produced an affidavit sworn by three witnesses to show that she was the legitimate daughter of a free Negro man and his Indian wife.

The century before the first Dutch slave-trading ship arrived in Virginia, therefore, had been an important and dramatic one for Africans in North America. They had experienced all of the hardships and some of the opportunities associated with transatlantic colonization. Arriving without choice, they had served where necessary and escaped where possible, proving to be every bit as opportunistic and independent as those around them. Isolated at outposts in Florida and New Mexico, they were cut off from ancestors in Africa and from most of their black compatriots on the expanding plantations of tropical America. These pioneers, few in number and spread out across the northern fringes of Spain's vast New World empire, inter-married along the way with the Africans, Europeans, and Indians whom they encountered in their amazing travels. Descendants of Gomez and Isabel and other early arrivals would live on in all the races of North America.

CHAPTER 2

The Uncertain Century

DURING THE FIRST HALF of the sixteenth century, while Gomez and Esteban encountered the wilderness of America, Europe was shaken by a religious upheaval. The disruption was so large that its shock waves had a lasting influence on all parts of the Atlantic world, including Africa and North America. Members of Europe's Catholic church, led by a German minister named Martin Luther, "protested" against practices of the established priesthood and challenged the authority of the Pope. These dissenters, called Protestants, broke away from the Catholic church in Rome and organized their own Christian churches. Their mass movement, aiming to "reform" Christianity to a purer and simpler pattern of earlier times, became known as the Reformation. Encouraged by the theologian John Calvin in Geneva, this rebellion against papal authority soon gained its strongest support in northern Europe.

There were more than religious motivations for defying papal power in Rome. The Catholic church was also a major economic and political force across Europe. Its large cathedrals and numerous monasteries made it a dominant landholder throughout the continent, and the Pope supported, and benefited from, the enormous spoils that flowed to Europe as a result of Spanish conquest in the New World. Both England and the Netherlands, two lands caught up in the Reformation, were small countries with excellent ports and long seagoing traditions. By the second half of the sixteenth century they each had enough ships and sailors, backed by private capital and encouraged by government leaders, to dare to challenge the awesome sea power of Catholic Spain. The Protestant Reformation's ideas about humanity's relationship to God and about papal authority added a religious and political dimension to this challenge.

Defending its economic power and its religious ties, Spain emerged as the leader of an extended "Counter-Reformation," and by the 1580s this struggle had erupted into international warfare in Europe. Among the Dutch, the northern provinces rebelled successfully against Spanish control (becoming the country we know as Holland or the Netherlands). Among the English, Queen Elizabeth's seamen, led by Sir Francis Drake, repelled a huge invasion by an armada of Spanish ships in 1588. Emboldened by such triumphs and jealous of Spanish and Portuguese success overseas, Dutch and English sea captains became increasingly active in Atlantic waters and beyond.

As a result, these religious and political rivalries in Europe took on a much wider and more lasting significance, reaching out to touch and shape the lives of many distant peoples, including early African Americans. Reformation rivalries helped determine where Africans would be transported in the New World and by whom, as well as which new languages they would hear and what forms of Christianity they would encounter. Most importantly, these struggles meant that for an entire uncertain century, from the 1560s to the 1660s and beyond, it was by no means clear how many Africans would reach North America or what their exact status would be when they arrived.

One way for Englishmen to gain access to Spain's closely guarded dominions and profits in the New World was to seek a role in shipping non-Christians between Africa and Latin America. Englishmen first tried transporting Africans across the Atlantic for gain in the 1560s, when an Elizabethan "sea dog" named John Hawkins made several slaving voyages from Africa to the Caribbean. Spanish reluctance, not English scruples, cut short this approach. Alternative ways for England to undermine the powerful Spaniards involved plundering their gold fleet in the waters of the Gulf Stream, or—even more dangerously— attacking their Central American ports and inciting discontented Indians and enslaved Africans to revolt against their Spanish overlords. Raiding Panama for treasure in 1572, Francis Drake received valuable aid from the so-called "Cimarrons," several thousand "valiant" Negroes living in the mountains who had, according to one English account, "fled from their cruel masters the Spaniards."

When Drake returned to the Spanish Caribbean on a similar mission in 1585, his countryman, Sir Walter Raleigh, sent a related expedition to the Atlantic Coast. Raleigh's men established an outpost at Roanoke Island. The spot (in modern-day North Carolina) was not far from Florida and was protected by the Outer Banks. From there, the colonists hoped to support raids against the Spaniards. In addition, the Protestant Englishmen intended to treat neighboring Indians and imported Africans with greater respect and humanity than their Catholic rivals had shown. The opportunity came sooner than they expected. Drake, having narrowly missed the Spanish treasure fleet, attacked several major Spanish ports, siding openly with local Cimarrons and embittered slaves. In Santo Domingo and Cartagena he extracted huge ransoms, captured valuable ships, and liberated hundreds of enslaved men and women—Indians, Africans, Turks, and Moors. Frightened Spanish officials reported "the pains he took to carry off launches and frigates, implements, locks and all sorts of hardware and negro laborours who in his country are free."

Drake's next stop was at St. Augustine, where his men attacked the fort and encouraged local Indians to burn the town. The victorious little fleet, carrying people from three different continents, then headed north up the coast to Roanoke. Three black men who remained behind at St. Augustine confirmed to authorities that their liberator "meant to leave all the negroes he had in a fort and settlement established . . . by the English who went there a year ago." But when Drake reached Roanoke in June 1586, he found the officers and men ready to give up their enterprise as a failure. Before he could unload his newly freed reinforcements and captured hardware, a summer storm scattered his fleet from its unprotected anchorage. Within days Drake sailed for England in his remaining ships, taking most of the garrison with him. A further settlement effort on the same spot the following year with more than 100 new colonists had disappeared by 1590, largely because boats carrying much-needed supplies were held in England to help resist the Spanish Armada.

The real mystery of this so-called "Lost Colony" is not what became of the English settlers; evidence suggests that most were absorbed peacefully into neighboring tribes. Instead, the most fascinating, and unanswerable, question concerns several hundred ex-slaves from the Caribbean. These people, mostly Africans, apparently vanished in the sudden storm, and records give no indication of their fate. But one wonders: What might have become of these "lost colonists" if they had managed to go ashore before the tempest struck? They would certainly have been put to work along with everyone else, for the outpost was short on supplies and needed additional hands. But the English, to score a propaganda victory, might have gone out of their way to convert these men and women to the Protestant religion and to make sure they lived more freely than under Spanish rule. Grateful for liberation and relative independence, these new-comers might have served in future Caribbean ventures, eager to gain revenge upon the Spanish, liberate fellow Africans, and share in possible spoils.

Who knows what might have been different if these early African Americans had not been lost at sea? Establishing new families and new loyalties, they might have pushed Protestant colonization policy toward tolerance of non-Europeans and conversion of non-Christians. Conceivably, they might have made Roanoke and future American outposts into beacons of liberation for Africans thrown into the caldron of Spanish plantation slavery in the tropics. But this was not to be. Ironically, within several generations enslaved Africans along the Atlantic Coast were beginning to look longingly toward St. Augustine as a small haven of comparative freedom.

However, this transition to rigid and unwavering racial enslavement in North America still lay in the future. Black arrivals before 1680, several thousand in number, came from varied backgrounds and often had extensive Caribbean experience. Most had been denied their freedom in the West Indies and had been forced to work as slaves, but this did not mean that their status was fixed for life in the fledgling colonies of the mainland. Frequently they spoke one or more European languages; often they were of mixed European and African ancestry. They entered a world where religious identity and the practical demands of daily survival still counted for far more than one's physical appearance or ethnic background. Between 1600 and the 1670s, the status of Africans in North America remained varied and uncertain, as the Protestant English and Dutch pushed to establish new settlements along a coastline that the Spanish had once claimed as their own.

In 1609, the Dutch laid claim to the area now known as New York when Henry Hudson sailed up the river that now bears his name. Their colony, called New Netherland, began as a fur trading outpost, and African Americans appeared there aboard the earliest ships. Juan Rodrigues, for example, was a mulatto sailor from the West Indies who arrived in the Hudson River Valley in the spring of 1612 aboard the Dutch ship *Jonge Tobias* under Captain Mossel. He may have jumped ship, or he may have been sent ashore secretly by his captain to steer the profitable commerce in furs away from competing traders. In either case, he disappeared into the forest carrying a musket and a sword for protection and 80 hatchets and some knives as potential trade goods. Rodrigues emerged the following year, having learned enough of the local Indian language to make himself valuable to the first ship of the season. He was recruited as an interpreter and trader by the captain of the *Fortuyn*, despite the protests of Captain Mossel, who arrived several weeks later.

By 1628, the Dutch had constructed a crude fort at the tip of Manhattan Island. They planned to import enslaved Africans to augment the supply of farm laborers in the little village of New Amsterdam, which had a population of fewer than 300 people. Several years later, the Dutch West India Company imported additional slaves from the Caribbean to rebuild the fort, and by 1639, a company map showed a slave camp five miles north of the town housing newcomers from the West Indies. Though most black settlers were legally enslaved and some apparently lived in a separate settlement, these few initial Afro-Dutch residents did not lead a life totally apart from other colonists in New Amsterdam. Some were granted "half-freedom" (they lived independently but continued to pay an annual tax); others were manumitted, or freed, by their owners and possessed their own land and labor. Indeed, it was possible for a European woman to work for an African freeman as an indentured servant.

Early Dutch records make clear that blacks were active in the courts. In June 1639, for example, a freeman named Pedro Negretto, who worked as a day laborer alongside Dutch farmhands, sued Jan Celes for failing to pay him for taking care of his hogs. Similarly, religious documents show that the few Africans who professed Christianity were permitted to marry within the Dutch Reformed church. Among fifty marriages recorded by the New Amsterdam church from 1639 to 1652, thirteen involved unions between black men and black women. In another, a man from Europe married a woman from Angola. When Indian wars threatened, as in 1641, Africans found themselves recruited by the governor and council to venture out in teams against Indian hunting parties. At such moments of danger to the whole community, Dutch officials were less interested in whether a man was free than in whether he was fast on his feet. To create these small squads, they issued an order to recruit "many Negroes from among the strongest and fleetest," arming each with "a hatchet and a half pike."

Though Holland steadily expanded its role in transporting Africans to the Americas, the population of New Netherland grew slowly at first. For the most part, the powerful Dutch confined their major traffic to the burgeoning plantation economies of the South Atlantic. They focused particularly on Portuguese Brazil, seizing temporary control there in 1637. They also took from the Portuguese several ports in Africa (Elmina on the Gold Coast and Luanda in Angola), and soon they were transporting 2,500 Africans per year west across the South Atlantic. A few of these people eventually ended up in New Amsterdam, as suggested by the presence in the records of such names as Paulo d'Angola, Simon Congo, and Anthony Portuguese.

In 1654, the Dutch lost control of Brazil, where they had been shipping thousands of Africans, so distant New Netherland suddenly became a more attractive destination for Dutch slavers from the South Atlantic. The first shipload of several hundred people brought directly from Africa arrived at the mouth of the Hudson in 1655. More shipments followed, and many of the enslaved passengers were promptly resold to English planters in the Chesapeake colonies seeking additional workers. By this time, the Dutch had made peace with the Spanish and found themselves at war with their former ally, England. In 1664, when the English seized New Netherland and renamed it New York, there may have been as many as 700 Dutch-speaking black residents in a population of 9,000. The Dutch soon turned their colonizing attention to other places— such as South Africa, where they had established a colony at the Cape of Good Hope in 1652.

It would be the English who expanded their hold on the Atlantic Coast of North America and steadily increased the number of blacks living there. As more black newcomers appeared in the English mainland colonies, racial designations gradually took on new significance. Eventually, legal codes would impose hereditary enslavement (that is, the condition of slavery was passed from parents to children); and profit-conscious traders would undertake the importation of slaves directly from Africa.

An early muster roll from the Plymouth Colony in New England, founded by the Pilgrims in 1620, shows that at least one African, "blackamoor" (the old English term for a dark-skinned African), was present in the community by the early 1630s and was serving in the militia. The journal of John Winthrop, governor of the larger Massachusetts Bay Colony (founded in 1630), makes clear that in 1638, not long after the English defeat of the neighboring Pequot Indians, a Boston sea captain carried Native American captives to the West Indies and brought back "salt, cotton, tobacco, and Negroes." Six years later, in 1644, Boston merchants sent several ships directly to the West African coast, a small beginning to a pattern of New England slave trading that would continue for a century and a half.

At the start of the seventh century, Christian Europeans still tended to see political and religious, not physical, differences as the key divisions among mankind. Enemies in foreign wars and adherents to different faiths could be captured and enslaved. For this reason, John Smith, a leader of the English colony at Jamestown, had been forced briefly into slavery by the Muslims when fighting in Eastern Europe as a young man; "infidel" Pequots who opposed Winthrop's men in New England were sold into bondage in the Caribbean. Such enslavement was not always for life; conversion to the religion of the captor and other forms of good behavior could result in freedom. A law passed in the colony of Rhode Island in 1652 even attempted to limit the term of involuntary servitude to ten years.

By mid-century, however, the condition of unfree colonists in North America had started to change. In the older colonies of the Spanish New World to the south, a pattern of hereditary servitude based upon race had long ago evolved into a powerful and irresistible system of exploitation. Now, slowly, this destructive institution began to gain a substantial foothold in the small colonies of the North American mainland as well. Its emergence would have a devastating effect on the next genera-tion of Africans to cross the Atlantic, and upon all of their descendants for several long centuries to come.

CHAPTER 3

The Terrible Transformation

DURING THE SECOND half of the seventeenth century, a terrible transformation, the enslavement of people solely on the basis of race, occurred in the lives of African Americans living in North America. These newcomers still numbered only a few thousand, but the bitter reversals they experienced—first subtle, then drastic—would shape the lives of all those who followed them, generation after generation.

Like most huge changes, the imposition of hereditary race slavery was gradual, taking hold by degrees over many decades. It proceeded slowly, in much the same way that winter follows fall. On any given day, in any given place, people can argue about local weather conditions. "Is it getting colder?" "Will it warm up again this week?" The shift may come early in some places, later in others. But eventually, it occurs all across the land. By January, people shiver and think back to September, agreeing that "it is definitely colder now." In 1700, a seventy-year-old African American could look back half a century to 1650 and shiver, knowing that conditions had definitely changed for the worse.

Some people had experienced the first cold winds of enslavement well before 1650; others would escape the chilling blast well after 1700. The timing and nature of the change varied considerably from colony to colony, and even from family to family. Gradually, the terrible transformation took on a momentum of its own, numbing and burdening everything in its path, like a disastrous winter storm. Unlike the changing seasons, however, the encroachment of racial slavery in the colonies of North America was certainly not a natural process. It was highly unnatural—the work of powerful competitive governments and many thousands of human beings spread out across the Atlantic world. Nor was it inevitable that people's legal status would come to depend upon their racial background and that the condition of slavery would be passed down from parent to child. Numerous factors combined to bring about this disastrous shift. It is worth exploring how all these human forces swirled together during the decades after 1650, to create an enormously destructive storm.

Consider the situation at mid-century along the Atlantic Coast. Except for St. Augustine in Florida, there were no colonial settlements south of Chesapeake Bay. The English and Dutch colonies remained extremely small. As growing communities, they felt a steady need for additional hands, but their first priority was to add persons of their own religion and nationality. Many newcomers labored for others, but most of them were "indentured"—they had signed contracts to work under fixed conditions for a limited number of years. Their term could be shortened for good service or lengthened for disobeying the laws, but when their indenture expired they looked forward to having land of their own. Ships sailing back to England and Holland regularly carried letters describing the pluses and minuses of each colony. As a result of this continuous feedback, European migrants learned to avoid the settlements that had the longest indentures, the poorest working conditions, and the least amount of available land.

Conditions in the Caribbean and Latin America were strikingly different. There, for well over a century, Spanish and Portuguese colonizers had enslaved "infidels": first Indians and then Africans. At first, they relied for justification upon the Mediterranean tradition that persons of a different religion, or persons captured in war, could be enslaved for life. But hidden in this idea of slavery was the notion that persons who converted to Christianity should receive their freedom. Wealthy planters in the tropics, afraid that their cheap labor would be taken away from them because of this loophole, changed the reasoning behind their exploitation. Even persons who could prove that they were not captured in war and that they accepted the Catholic faith still could not change their appearance, any more than a leopard can change its spots. So by making color the key factor behind enslavement, dark-skinned people brought from Africa to work in silver mines and on sugar plantations could be exploited for life. Indeed, the servitude could be made hereditary, so enslaved people's children automatically inherited the same unfree status.

By 1650, hereditary enslavement based upon color, not upon religion, was a bitter reality in the older Catholic colonies of the New World. But this cruel and self-perpetuating system had not yet taken firm hold in North America for a variety of reasons. The same anti-Catholic propaganda that had led Sir Francis Drake to liberate Negro slaves in Central America in the 1580s still prompted many colonists to believe that it was the Protestant mission to convert non-Europeans rather than enslave them. In 1645, authorities in Massachusetts ordered a New Hampshire resident to give up a black worker he had purchased in Boston; they argued that the man had been stolen from his home, not captured in war, and therefore should be returned to Africa. Seven years later, Rhode Island officials passed a law that attempted to limit all involuntary servitude to ten years.

Apart from such moral concerns, there were simple matters of cost and practicality. Workers subject to longer terms and coming from further away would require a larger initial investment. Consider a 1648 document from York County, Virginia, showing the market values for persons working for James Stone (estimated in terms of pounds of tobacco):

Francis Bomley for 6 yeares	1500
John Thackstone for 3 yeares	1300
Susan Davis for 3 yeares	1000
Emaniell a Negro man	2000
Roger Stone 3 yeares	1300
Mingo a Negro man	2000

Among all six, Susan had the lowest value. She may have been less strong in the tobacco field, and as a woman she ran a greater risk of early death because of the dangers of childbirth. Hence John and Roger, the other English servants with three-year terms, commanded a higher value. Francis, whose term was twice as long, was not worth twice as much. Life expectancy was short for everyone in early Virginia, so he might not live to complete his term. The two black workers, Emaniell and Mingo, clearly had longer terms, perhaps even for life, and they also had the highest value. If they each lived for another 20 years, they represented a bargain for Mr. Stone, but if they died young, perhaps even before they had fully learned the language, their value as workers proved far less. From Stone's point of view they represented a risky and expensive investment at best.

By 1650, however, conditions were already beginning to change. For one thing, both the Dutch and the English had started using enslaved Africans to produce sugar in the Caribbean and the tropics. English experiments at Barbados and Providence Island showed that Protestant investors could easily overcome their moral scruples. Large profits could be made if foreign rivals could be held in check. After agreeing to peace with Spain and giving up control of Northeast Brazil at mid-century, Dutch slave traders were actively looking for new markets. In England, after Charles II was restored to the throne in 1660, he rewarded supporters by creating the Royal African Company to enter aggressively into the slave trade. The English king also chartered a new colony in Carolina. He hoped it would be close enough to the Spanish in Florida and the Caribbean to challenge them in economic and military terms. Many of the first English settlers in Carolina after 1670 came from Barbados. They brought enslaved Africans with them. They also brought the beginnings of a legal code and a social system that accepted race slavery.

While new colonies with a greater acceptance of race slavery were being founded, the older colonies continued to grow. Early in the seventeenth century no tiny North American port could absorb several hundred workers arriving at one time on a large ship. Most Africans—such as those reaching Jamestown in 1619—arrived several dozen at a time aboard small boats and privateers from the Caribbean. Like Emaniell and Mingo on the farm of James Stone, they tended to mix with other unfree workers on small plantations. All of these servants, no matter what their origin, could hope to obtain their own land and the personal independence that goes with private property. In 1645, in Northampton County on Virginia's Eastern Shore, Captain Philip Taylor, after complaining that "Anthony the negro" did not work hard enough for him, agreed to set aside part of the cornfield where they worked as Anthony's plot. "I am very glad of it," the black man told a local clerk; "now I know myne owne ground and I will worke when I please and play when I please."

Anthony and Mary Johnson had also gained their own property in Northampton County before 1650. He had arrived in Virginia in 1621, aboard the *James*, and was cited on early lists as "Antonio a Negro." He was put to work on the tobacco plantation of Edward Bennett, with more than fifty other people. All except five were killed the following March, when local Indians struck back against the foreigners who were invading their land. Antonio was one of the lucky survivors. He became increasingly English in his ways, eventually gaining his freedom and moving to the Eastern Shore, where he was known as Anthony Johnson. Along the way, he married "Mary a Negro Woman," who had arrived in 1622 aboard the *Margrett and John*, and they raised at least four children, gaining respect for their "hard labor and known service," according to the court records of Northampton County.

By the 1650s, Anthony and Mary Johnson owned a farm of 250 acres, and their married sons, John and Richard, farmed adjoining tracts of 450 and 100 acres respectively. In the 1660s, the whole Johnson clan pulled up stakes and moved north into Maryland, where the aging Anthony leased a 300-acre farm called "Tonies Vineyard" until his death. His widow Mary, in her will of 1672, distributed a cow to each of her grandsons, including John, Jr., the son of John and Susanna Johnson. Five years later, when John, Jr., purchased a 44-acre farm for himself, he named the homestead Angola, which suggests that his grand-parents had been born in Africa and had kept alive stories of their homeland within the family. But within thirty years, John, Jr., had died without an heir, and the entire Johnson family had disappeared from the colonial records. If we knew their fate, it might tell us more about the terrible transformation that was going on around them.

Gradually, it was becoming harder to obtain English labor in the mainland colonies. Civil war and a great plague reduced England's population, and the Great Fire of London created fresh demands for workers at home. Stiff penalties were imposed on sea captains who grabbed young people in England and sold them in the colonies as indentured servants. (This common practice was given a new name: "kidnapping.") English servants already at work in the colonies demanded shorter indentures, better working conditions, and suitable farmland when their contracts expired. Officials feared they would lose future English recruits to rival colonies if bad publicity filtered back to Europe, so they could not ignore this pressure, even when it undermined colonial profits.

Nor could colonial planters turn instead to Indian labor. Native Americans captured in frontier wars continued to be enslaved, but each act of aggression by European colonists made future diplomacy with neighboring Indians more difficult. Native American captives could easily escape into the familiar wilderness and return to their original tribe. Besides, their numbers were limited. African Americans, in contrast, were thousands of miles from their homeland, and their availability increased as the scope of the Atlantic slave trade expanded. More European countries competed to transport and exploit African labor; more West African leaders proved willing to engage in profitable trade with them; more New World planters had the money to purchase new workers from across the ocean. It seemed as though every decade the ships became larger, the contacts more regular, the departures more frequent, the routes more familiar, the sales more efficient.

As the size and efficiency of this brutal traffic increased, so did its rewards for European investors. Their ruthless competition pushed up the volume of transatlantic trade from Africa and drove down the relative cost of individual Africans in the New World at a time when the price of labor from Europe was rising. As their profits increased, slave merchants and their captains continued to look for fresh markets. North America, on the fringe of this expanding and infamous Atlantic system, represented a likely target. As the small mainland colonies grew and their trade with one another and with England increased, their capacity to purchase large numbers of new laborers from overseas expanded. By the end of the century, Africans were arriving aboard large ships directly from Africa as well as on smaller boats from the West Indies. In 1698, the monopoly held by England's Royal African Company on this transatlantic business came to an end, and independent traders from England and the colonies stepped up their voyages, intending to capture a share of the profits.

All these large and gradual changes would still not have brought about the terrible transformation to race slavery, had it not been for several other crucial factors. One ingredient was the mounting fear among colonial leaders regarding signs of discontent and cooperation among poor and unfree colonists of all sorts. Europeans and Africans worked together, intermarried, ran away together, and shared common resentments toward the well-to-do. Both groups were involved in a series of bitter strikes and servant uprisings among tobacco pickers in Virginia, culminating in an open rebellion in 1676. Greatly outnumbered by these armed workers, authorities were quick to sense the need to divide their labor force in order to control it. Stressing cultural and ethnic divisions would be one way to do that.

A second crucial ingredient contributing to worsening conditions was the total lack of feedback within the stream of African arrivals. If masters mistreated their English servants, word of such abuses could reach England and influence future migration. Whether this information traveled by letter or by word of mouth, it provided an incentive for fair treatment that did not exist for migrants brought from Africa. Once deported across the Atlantic, Africans had no prospect of returning to their homeland, and few European sailors possessed the will, or the language skill, to carry the full story of New World enslavement back to the seaports of West Africa. Therefore, when an English master misused his African workers, it had no influence upon the future supply of labor from that continent. He was therefore tempted to hold them for life, reasoning that they had been enslaved for life long before he ever saw them. Once they were held for life, he could not extend their term of service for bad behavior (the usual punishment for indentured servants), so he resorted increasingly to harsh physical punishments, knowing that this year's brutality would not effect next year's supply of African labor.

Lifetime servitude could be enforced only by removing the prospect that a person might gain freedom through Christian conversion. One approach was to outlaw this traditional route to freedom. As early as 1664, a Maryland statute specified that Christian baptism could have no effect upon the legal status of a slave. A more sweeping solution, however, involved removing religion altogether as a factor in determining servitude. Therefore, a third and fundamental key to the terrible transformation was the shift from changeable spiritual faith to unchangeable physical appearance as a measure of status. Increasingly, the dominant English came to view Africans not as "heathen people" but as "black people." They began, for the first time, to describe themselves not as Christians but as whites. And they gradually wrote this shift into their colonial laws. Within a generation, the English definition of who could be made a slave had shifted from someone who was not a Christian to someone who was not European in appearance. Indeed, the transition for self-interested Englishmen went further. It was a small but momentous step from saying that black persons *could* be enslaved to saying that Negroes *should* be enslaved. One Christian minister was dismayed by this rapid change to slavery based on race: "These two words, *Negro* and *Slave*," wrote the Reverend Morgan Godwyn in 1680, are "by custom grown Homogeneous and Convertible"—that is, interchangeable.

As if this momentous shift were not enough, it was accompanied by another. Those who wrote the colonial laws not only moved to make slavery *racial*; they also made it *hereditary*. Under English common law, a child inherited the legal status of the father. As Virginia officials put it when looking into the case of Elizabeth Key in 1655: "By the Comon Law the Child of a Woman slave begott by a freeman ought to bee free." Elizabeth, called Black Bess by her neighbors, was the mulatto daughter of Thomas Key and his Negro servant. As a child, she had been indentured by her father for nine years to Colonel Humphrey Higginson, but after Thomas Key died others had attempted to extend her term of service indefinitely.

Now Bess was in her mid-twenties and anxious to prove her free status in court before marrying William Greensted. After hearing sworn testimony, the authorities ruled that "the said Elizabeth ought to bee free and that her last Master should give her Corne and Cloathes and give her satisfaction for the time shee hath served longer than Shee ought to have done." Bess did indeed have the same status as her father and was free to marry William. But within seven years that option had been removed. Faced with similar cases of "whether children got by any Englishman upon a negro woman should be slave or Free," the Virginia Assembly in 1662 decided in favor of the master demanding service rather than the child claiming freedom. In this special circumstance, the Assembly ignored all English precedents that children inherited the name and status of their father. Instead, the men in the colonial legislature declared that all such children "borne in this country shal be held bond or free only according to the condition of the mother." In Virginia, and soon elsewhere, the children of slave mothers would be slaves forever.

Now the terrible transformation was almost complete, with the colony of Virginia leading the way. An additional legal sleight of hand by the land-hungry Virginia gentry helped speed the process. For several generations, as an incentive toward immigration, newcomers had received title to a parcel of land, called a "headright," for every family member or European servant they brought to the struggling colony.

By expanding this system to include Africans, self-interested planter-magistrates, who were rich enough to make the initial investment in enslaved workers, managed to obtain free land, as well as valuable labor, every time they purchased an African worker.

In the decades before 1700, therefore, the number of African arrivals began to increase, and the situation of African Americans became increasingly precarious and bleak. Sarah Driggus, an African-American woman who had been born free during the middle of the 17th century, protested to a Maryland court in 1688 that she was now being regarded as a slave. Many others of her generation were feeling similar pressures and filing similar protests. But fewer and fewer of them were being heard. The long winter of racial enslavement was closing in over the English colonies of North America.

CHAPTER 4

A Nation of Newcomers

IN 1976, THE African-American writer Alex Haley traced the story of his black family in the popular book *Roots*. He discovered that his "furthest-back-person" in America was Kunte Kinte, a Gambian who had been brought in chains from West Africa to Annapolis, Maryland, in the 1760s aboard the English slave ship *Lord Ligonier*. Haley (who also wrote the powerful *Autobiography of Malcolm X*) was fortunate in knowing the name of his first American forebear and in being able to locate the exact ship on which he arrived. But the facts themselves are remarkably typical. On average, the furthest-back New World ancestor for any African American today would have reached these shores shortly before the American Revolution, just as Kunte Kinte did. (By comparison, the largest migrations of Europeans and Asians to the United States began in the late 19th century and grew larger in the twentieth century. So the average white resident of the United States has a far shorter American ancestry, as does the average Asian-American citizen.)

Newcomers like Kunte Kinte were part of a large forced migration that started in earnest shortly before 1700 and ended, for the most part, shortly after 1800. By the time the government of the young United States prohibited further importation of enslaved Africans in 1807, well over 600,000 people had been brought to North America directly from Africa or indirectly via the Caribbean. (Most of these people were transported to English-speaking settlements on the East Coast, although some entered Florida and Louisiana; many fewer entered Canada and the Spanish Southwest.) Nearly 200,000 of these enslaved people arrived during the final generation of the slave trade, between 1776 and 1807. This means that more than 400,000 Africans reached North America during the century stretching between 1675 and 1775. They were described at the time as "Saltwater Negroes," Africans who had endured the Atlantic crossing. This diverse group of men and women occupies an important place in American history.

Even though these black ancestors arrived in North America *early* compared to most white ancestors, they arrived *late* in comparison with Africans elsewhere in the New World. By 1700, the slave trade from Africa had been underway for two centuries to the Caribbean and Latin America, although it was only beginning to shape North American society. In addition, these ancestors represent a surprisingly small part—less than seven percent—of the entire transatlantic movement from Africa. All told, well over twelve million people endured this brutal traffic to the New World, and several million more perished during the so-called Middle Passage.

Moreover, even within the British portion of the vast African trade, Africans sent to North American ports represented only a small portion of the total exodus. Between 1690 and 1807,

English captains deported nearly 2.75 million slaves from Africa. Most were sold in foreign ports, but English planters on the tiny island of Barbados purchased more African slaves than all the mainland British colonies combined, and English-controlled Jamaica absorbed fully twice as many workers. Finally, unlike their countrymen dispersed through the sugar cultures of the tropics, the Africans transported to North America managed to live longer on average and bear more children. Almost from the start, the number of births regularly exceeded the number of deaths in most places over the course of each year, meaning that the black population grew steadily, regardless of new importations from Africa.

The conditions faced by these saltwater slaves were less horrendous than those encountered by their black contemporaries entering the sugar colonies of Latin America. But they were decidedly worse than those faced by the few thousand Africans reaching North America before 1675 (or by the numerous Europeans who arrived in increasing numbers throughout the 18th century). By 1700, conditions were changing dramatically. Diverse forces had combined in the late seventeenth century to slowly and terribly transform the status of African arrivals from bad to worse.

Two further adjustments assured that this system of race-based exploitation would endure across North America for generations—and in some regions for more than 150 years. The first shift involved the creation of strict legal codes in one colony after another, spelling out the organized practice of discrimination and giving it the full force of the law. Wealthy white assemblymen, representing the landowning gentry who would benefit the most financially from these changes, enacted statutes that destroyed the legal standing of African Americans.

The laws of the land they had entered viewed them not as humans with rights but as property to be controlled by others. Specific statutes prohibited enslaved blacks from earning wages, moving about freely, congregating in groups, seeking education, marrying whites, carrying firearms, resisting punishment, or testifying in court. In 1705, Virginia legislators gathered diverse laws aimed against blacks into a single comprehensive "slave code," and other colonies followed this example.

English colonists took another step as well—less formal but equally destructive. Brutal and dehumanizing treatment of African newcomers was approved not only in the colonial courts of law, but also in the broad court of white public opinion. The phenomenon all Americans know as "racism"—which peaked in the nineteenth century and lingers even at the start of the twenty-first century—first emerged as a solid feature of North American society in the early eighteenth century. In Boston, the prominent Puritan minister Cotton Mather (himself a slave-holder) generalized about what he viewed as the "stupidity" of Negroes. In 1701, another Bostonian refused to free his African slave on the grounds that the "character" of every black person was innately deficient. In a bitterly racist poem, merchant John Saffin denounced African men as lustful and murderous, "Cowardly and cruel . . . , Prone to Revenge . . . , False and Rude." Here were all the ingredients of the degrading racist stereotype that would be mouthed by so many future generations of white Americans, north and south.

Unquestionably, signs of European prejudice and discrimination toward Indians and Africans had been present in the English colonies from the start. But this poisonous pattern of mistrust and abuse became widespread and central within the culture only after 1700, as race slavery rapidly expanded.

One indication of this racism was the increased hostility toward marriages between Africans and Europeans. Such interracial unions became illegal in Virginia in 1691, in Massachusetts in 1705, in Maryland in 1715, and soon after in most other colonies.

Another indication was the sharp prejudice exhibited toward free blacks. A law passed in Virginia in 1699 required black persons receiving their freedom to leave the colony within six months. The assembly argued that additional free blacks would represent "great inconveniences . . . by their either entertaining negro slaves . . . , or receiving stolen goods, or being grown old bringing a charge upon the country."

Ironically, as the situation worsened and the options diminished for African Americans, their population in certain English mainland colonies rose dramatically. In the 40 years between 1680 and 1720, the proportion of blacks in Virginia's population jumped from 7 percent to 30 percent, as white landowners shifted from a labor system of indentured servitude to one of chattel slavery. "They import so many Negros hither," observed planter William Byrd II, "that I fear this Colony will some time or other be confirmed by the Name of New Guinea." In South Carolina during the same four decades the African increase was even more pronounced: from seventeen percent to seventy percent. "Carolina," commented Swiss newcomer Samuel Dyssli in 1737, "looks more like a negro country than like a country settled by white people." During the 1740s and 1750s, an average of 5,000 Africans per year were being sold into bondage on American docks. In 1760, Virginia had more than 130,000 black residents, and fifteen years later the number had jumped beyond 185,000. By the eve of the American Revolution, the proportion of African Americans in the population of North America was higher than it would ever be in any subsequent generation.

Several hundred thousand Africans appear as nameless statistics in ship logs and port records from eighteenth-century North America. Only in exceptional cases can we reconstruct the life of an individual saltwater slave with much certainty. Ayuba Suleiman Diallo, best known as Job ben Solomon, is one such exception. He was born around 1702 to Tanomata, the wife of a Fula high priest named Solomon Diallo in the region of Bondou between the Senegal and Gambia rivers of West Africa, more than 200 miles inland from the Atlantic Ocean.

Raised as a Muslim, Job could read and write Arabic easily; by the time he was fifteen this exceptional student had committed the Koran to memory and could copy it by heart. His education proved his salvation after March 1, 1731, when he suddenly found himself in chains aboard an English slave ship. He was no stranger to the slave trade, for French captains on the Senegal and English captains on the Gambia further south bartered regularly for captives, and merchant families like the Diallos often took advantage of this stiff competition to drive profitable bargains. Indeed, by his own later account, Job had just sold two persons into slavery in exchange for twenty-eight cattle. He was beginning the long trek home with his new herd when he was suddenly kidnapped by a group of Mandingo men and sold to an Englishman on the Gambia, Captain Pyke of the *Arabella*. Job sent a message to his wealthy father asking for help, but before the distant priest could ransom his son (by providing two replacement slaves), the *Arabella* had set sail across the Atlantic.

For Captain Pyke, the transit from Africa to America was the middle leg of a three-part voyage that began and ended in

England and was designed to bring profit to investors Henry and William Hunt.

But for the Africans crammed below decks, this "Middle Passage" was a terrifying one-way journey from which no one could expect to return. The voyage from James Fort on the Gambia River to Annapolis, Maryland, on Chesapeake Bay was long and hard, as Kunte Kinte would discover three decades later. The men and women were kept in separate, foul-smelling holds. They were given terrible food and almost no chance to move about. For some, the endless motion of the ship brought seasickness; for others, the constant chafing against hard boards created open sores that could not heal. The threat of infection and epidemic disease hung over the captives constantly, made worse by their crowded conditions and the daily changes in temperature below decks, from scorching heat to damp chill.

At times, for this cramped and weakened array of Africans, the mental suffering exceeded the physical pain. Each individual had been separated from family and friends and thrown together with strangers and, occasionally, enemies. Their captors appeared to be pale men with brutal ways and an unknown language. Their current location, future destination, and ultimate fate remained a mystery. Not everyone could endure this long, dark agony. When the crew, in its daily inspections, found that some had died, their bodies were literally "thrown to the sharks." This prompted further despair, and some, if they shared a common language, spoke of violent revolt. They were physically weakened, narrowly confined, and closely watched. Moreover, they were totally unarmed, uncertain of their whereabouts, and innocent of the workings of the large ship, so an uprising seemed nearly suicidal. Despite these odds, a shipload of passengers occasionally attempted to rebel. But most, however desperate, struggled simply to endure, praying to be saved from this nightmare into the unknown.

For Job ben Solomon, almost alone among more than 100,000 prisoners transported from the Senegambia region to the New World aboard British ships, this prayer would eventually be answered. When Pyke reached Annapolis, he turned over saltwater slaves to Vachell Denton, a local "factor," or agent, who was paid by merchant William Hunt of London to sell the *Arabella's* human cargo at a profit. When Denton put Job on the auction block, he was purchased for 45 pounds by Alexander Tolsey, a planter from Queen Anne's County. Job's new master attempted to change his name to Simon and put him to work picking tobacco and herding cattle. This latter task was a thoroughly familiar one, and it gave him time to pray regularly in the woods and also to plan an escape. But when he ran away in desperation, he was captured easily and confined to jail in the back of a local tavern. While there he was visited by an elderly saltwater slave who could still speak Wolof, Job's native language, and the old man explained to Job the full outlines of his predicament.

The ingenious young Fula now wrote a note in Arabic to his important father, explaining his dilemma and requesting Captain Pyke to deliver the letter on his next voyage to the Gambia River. Against all odds, Job sent it to Mr. Denton in Annapolis, who forwarded the curiosity to Mr. Hunt in London, who in turn showed a copy to friends until a translation was obtained from a professor of Arabic at Oxford University. Officials of the Royal African Company, including James Oglethorpe, the idealistic founder of the Georgia colony, took an immediate interest in the note. The author clearly had powerful relatives in Africa who might be of use in future trading ventures, if only the captive could be bought in Maryland and returned safely to Gambia. Tediously, the sum of forty-five pounds passed from Oglethorpe to Hunt to Denton to Tolsey, and by the spring of 1733 Job was aboard a ship sailing from Annapolis to London. During the eight-week voyage, between bouts of seasickness, he practiced his English and mastered the European alphabet.

In London, officials of the Royal African Company prepared a certificate "setting forth that Simon otherwise called Job the Gambia black lately brought from Maryland, is . . . to be a free man; and that he is at liberty to take his passage to Africa in any of the Company's ships." They assured Job they would avoid taking Muslim slaves in the future. In return, he agreed to assist them in their competition with the French to gain access to his homeland and its traffic in gold, gum, and non-Muslim slaves. He reached the Gambia River in August 1734, after four years away from Africa, and was met by Francis Moore, the Royal African Company's agent at James Fort.

Moore was eager to benefit from Job's return, so he sent a messenger to Bondou. The man returned in several weeks with disheartening news. According to Moore, he reported that Job's father had recently died and his prosperous country, once noted for its "numerous herds of large cattle," had been ravaged by such a terrible war "that there is not so much as one cow left in it." On top of all that, one of Job's wives had given him up for lost and had married another man. As Moore recorded in his journal, Job "wept grievously for his father's death, and the misfortunes of his country. He forgave his wife, and the man that had taken her; for, says he, Mr. Moore, she could not help thinking I was dead, for I was gone to a land from whence no Pholey [Fula] ever yet returned; therefore she is not to be blamed, nor the man neither."

Though Job ben Solomon's personal sorrows seemed heavy, his biographer rightly calls him "the fortunate slave." Thousands upon thousands were less fortunate, torn away from Africa unwillingly and sold into bondage overseas, with no hope of return. Some of these men and women had already been slaves in their own lands—captured in war, condemned for a crime, or purchased for a price. But they had been treated as people, not as property. They had been allowed to marry and raise families, and their children did not face continuous servitude. Captives deported across the ocean faced a new kind of slavery. They entered a system driven by enormous profits, tolerated by the Christian churches, bolstered by increasing racism, and backed by the full sanction of the law. Very few found ways to tell their story, but one who did was named Olaudah Equiano, who was seized with his sister at age eleven and shipped to Virginia via Barbados.

Equiano was apparently born in 1745 among the Ibo people living near the lower Niger River, an area under the loose control of the king of Benin. Like Job ben Solomon, Olaudah grew up in a slave-owning family. Like Job, he was captured in his native land and shipped to Chesapeake Bay, eventually gaining his freedom and making his way to England. Unlike Job, he did not return to Africa and become a participant in the slave trade from which he had escaped. Instead, he sailed extensively during the era of the American Revolution—to Jamaica, Portugal, Turkey, Greenland. He spoke frequently in Britain about the evils of slavery, and in 1789 he published a vivid autobiography, in which he described the circumstances of his arrival in the New World.

At last we came in sight of the island of Barbadoes, at which the whites on board gave a great shout, and made many signs of joy to us. We did not know what to think of this; but as the vessel drew nearer, we plainly saw the harbor, and other ships of different kinds and sizes, and we anchored amongst them, off Bridgetown. Many merchants and planters now came on board, though it was in the evening. They put us in separate parcels, and examined us attentively. They also made us jump, and pointed to the land, signifying we were to go there. We thought by this, we should be eaten by these ugly men, as they appeared to us; and, when soon after we were all put down under the deck again, there was much dread and trembling among us, and nothing but bitter cries to be heard all the night from these apprehensions, insomuch, that at last the white people got some old slaves from the land to pacify us. They told us we were not to be eaten, but to work, and were soon to go on land, where we should see many of our country people. This report eased us much. And sure enough, soon after we were landed, there came to us Africans of all languages.

We were conducted immediately to the merchant's yard, where we were all pent up together, like so many sheep in a fold, without regard to sex or age. As every object was new to me, everything I saw filled me with surprise. What struck me first, was, that the houses were built with bricks and stories, and in every other respect different from those I had seen in Africa.

We were not many days in the merchant's custody, before we were sold after their usual manner. . . . I now totally lost the small remains of comfort I had enjoyed in conversing with my countrymen; the women too, who used to wash and take care of me were all gone different ways, and I never saw one of them afterwards.

I stayed in this island for a few days, I believe it could not be above a fortnight, when I, and some few more slaves, that were not saleable amongst the rest, from very much fretting, were shipped off in a sloop for North America. On the passage we were better treated than when we were coming from Africa, and we had plenty of rice and fat pork. We were landed up a river a good way from the sea, about Virginia county, where we saw few or none of our native Africans, and not one soul who could talk to me. I was a few weeks weeding grass and gathering stones in a plantation; and at last my companions were distributed different ways, and only myself was left. I was now exceedingly miserable.

Those Africans like Equiano who were shipped to North America made up only one small portion of an enormous stream. But their numbers grew rapidly, particularly in the Southern colonies. Between 1770 and 1775, Charleston, South Carolina, was receiving 4,000 Africans per year. All of them were held for several weeks at the so-called pest house on Sullivan's Island, a quarantine station designed to prevent the arrival of epidemics from overseas. So many people arrived there that it has been called "the Ellis Island of black America." Yet unlike the Europeans who poured into New York City through Ellis Island in the late nineteenth and early twentieth centuries, the saltwater slaves of the eighteenth century could have little hope for a life that was more self-sufficient or humane than the one they left behind. No Statue of Liberty, with her Torch of Freedom upraised, welcomed these huddled and oppressed African newcomers, no beacon offered a promise of justice, well-being, and sanctuary from the world's storms. On the contrary, the storm had just begun.

5

A World of Work

MOST IMMIGRANTS COMING to North America arrive with high hopes. They expect to work hard, and they assume their efforts will somehow yield tangible rewards for themselves or their children. Over the centuries the dream has not always been fulfilled, but the dream exists. It did not exist, however, for Africans arriving in colonial North America after the terrible transformation. They had no choice in their deportation and no knowledge of their destination. From the hold of a slave ship, they could only speculate about the reason for their abduction and the nature of their impending fate.

What awaited them was a world of work—lifetimes of unending labor, rigidly controlled. Equiano and thousands of other people like him soon came to the realization that they were to be kept alive, but only in order to work. Their labor would benefit others, rather than themselves. They would be granted minimal food and clothing and shelter in exchange for their toil; there would be no wages and no possibility to save for a better future. Indeed, it seemed clear there would be no better future. The incentive for parents to work hard so that their children could enjoy a better life had been removed for almost all Africans by the terrible transformation to race slavery, which obliged each generation to inherit the same unfree status as the last.

The servitude facing African newcomers was the horrible outgrowth of unprecedented economic warfare on an international scale. With the rise of European exploration overseas, the battles for supremacy among a few rival monarchies had spread far beyond Europe. Their struggles to establish profitable colonies abroad took on new intensity after the religious Reformation divided Europe into competing Protestant and Catholic powers. By creating diverse colonial settlements, each country hoped to provide itself with a steady flow of resources—gold and silver, furs and fish, timber and tobacco, sugar and rice. At the same time, they would prevent rivals from obtaining access to the same goods, unless they were willing to pay a high price.

By 1700, mounting competition had led to the creation of numerous New World colonies, and during the 18th century rival European powers would establish additional outposts in all corners of North America. In successive generations the French colonized Louisiana, the English settled Georgia, the Spanish entered California, and the Russians laid claim to Alaska. Though very different in location and purpose, each new European settlement demanded a steady supply of labor in order to survive and grow as a profitable colony. In many places accessible to the transatlantic slave trade, it was Africans who filled that growing demand for labor during the century before the American Revolution.

Fig. 1: *The Spaniards who invaded the Southwest before 1600 took captive Indians south as slaves to work in the silver mines of New Spain. They also brought blacks and mulattoes north when they colonized New Mexico.*

Fig. 2: *During the seventeenth century, Dutch ships transported several thousand Africans to the New World each year. Most were enslaved on Brazilian and Caribbean sugar plantations, but a few hundred labored in New Amsterdam.*

Fig. 3: *Job ben Solomon has been called the "fortunate slave"
because he managed to return from Maryland to Gambia.
His remarkable story, illustrated with an engraving of the young
Muslim man, appeared in the June 1750 issue of* Gentleman's
Magazine.

Fig. 4: *This large drum, found in Virginia before 1753, resembles Ashanti instruments from Ghana and was probably created in the colony by an African familiar with that tradition. Some colonies banned slaves from using drums because they could be used to send messages.*

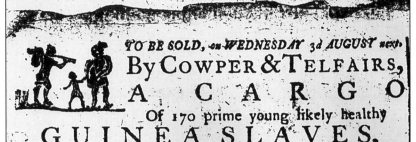

TO BE SOLD, on WEDNESDAY 3d AUGUST next,

By COWPER & TELFAIRS,

A CARGO

Of 170 prime young likely healthy

GUINEA SLAVES,

Juft imported, in the Bark Friends, William Rofs Mafter, directly from Angola.   Savannah, July 25, 1774.

To be Sold at Private Sale, any Time before the 18th of next Month.

THE PLANTATION, containing one hundred acres, on which the fubfcriber lives, very pleafantly fituated on Savannah River in fight of town. The terms of fale may be known by applying to
July 21, 1774   RICHARD WYLLY.

WANTED,

AN OVERSEER thoroughly qualified to undertake the fettlement of a River Swamp Plantation on the Alatamaha River. Any fuch perfon, who can bring proper recommendations, may hear of great encouragement by applying to   NATHANIEL HALL.

THE fubfcriber being under an abfolute neceffity of clofing his concerns without delay, gives this laft publick notice, that all perfons indebted to him by bond, note or otherwife, who do not difcharge the fame by the firft day of October next, will find their refpective obligations, &c in the hands of an Attorney to be fued for without diftinction. It is hoped thofe concerned will avail themfelves of this notice.
           PHILIP BOX.

RUN AWAY the 20th of May laft from John Forbes, Efq.'s plantation in St. John's parifh, TWO NEGROES, named BILLY and QUAMINA, of the Guinea Country, and fpeak good Englifh. Billy is lufty and well made, about 5 feet 10 or 11 inches high, of a black complection, has loft fome of his upper teeth, and had on when he went away a white negroe cloth jacket and trowfers of the fame. Quamina is ftout and well made, about 5 feet 10 or 11 inches high, very black, has his country marks on his face, had on when he went away a jacket, trowfers and robbin, of white negroe cloth. Whoever takes up faid Negroes, and deliver them to me at the above plantation, or to the Warden of the Work-Houfe in Savannah, fhall receive a reward of 20s. befides what the law allows.
           DAVIS AUSTIN.

Fig. 5: *African newcomers to America, such as those reaching Savannah from Angola in July 1774, would learn the strange language of their oppressors from earlier arrivals such as Billy and Quamina, who were said to "speak good English."*

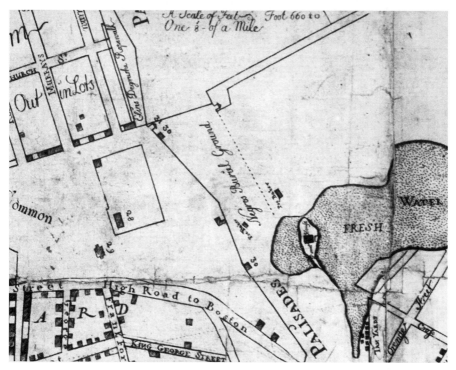

Fig. 6: *The location of the "Negros Burial Ground" is clearly marked on this 1755 map of New York City. During the nineteenth century there was extensive building in the area, and the site was forgotten until excavation work for a new federal office building in 1991 uncovered 420 human skeletons.*

An Address to the Atheist, By P. Wheatley at the age of
14 years. — 1767

Muse! where shall I begin the spacious field
To tell what curses unbelief doth yield?
Thou who dost daily feel his hand, and rod
Darest thou deny the Essence of a God!
If there's no heav'n, ah! whither wilt thou go,
Make thy Elysium in the shades below?
If there's no God from whom did all things spring
He made the greatest and minutest thing
Angelic ranks no less his Power display
Than the least mite scarce visible to day
With vast astonishment my soul is struck
Have reasoning powers thy darken'd breast forsook?
The Laws deep graven by the hand of God,
Seal'd with Immanuel's all-redeeming blood:
This second point thy folly dares deny
On thy devoted head for vengeance cry—
Turn then I pray thee from the dangerous road
Rise from the dust and seek the mighty God.
His is bright truth without a dark disguise
And his are wisdom's all beholding Eyes:
With labour'd snares our Adversary great
Withholds from us the Kingdom and the seat
Bliss weeping waits thee, in her arms to fly
To her own regions of felicity—
Perhaps thy ignorance will ask us where?
Go to the corner stone he will declare.
Thy heart in unbelief will harden'd grow
Tho' much indulg'd in vicious pleasure now—
Thou tak'st unusual means: the path forbear
Unkind to others, to thy self severe—
Methinks I see the consequence thou'rt blind
Thy unbelief disturbs the peaceful Mind.

Fig. 7: Phillis Wheatley wrote "An Address to the Atheist" when she
was fourteen years old. Wheatley was among those black Americans
who began to embrace Christianity in increasing numbers.

SIR,

THE efforts made by the legiflative of this province in their laft feffions to free themfelves from flavery, gave us, who are in that deplorable ftate, a high degree of fatisfaction. We expect great things from men who have made fuch a noble ftand againft the defigns of their *fellow-men* to enflave them. We cannot but wifh and hope Sir, that you will have the fame grand object, we mean civil and religious liberty, in view in your next feffion. The divine fpirit of *freedom*, feems to fire every humane breaft on this continent, except fuch as are bribed to affift in executing the execrable plan.

WE are very fenfible that it would be highly detrimental to our prefent mafters, if we were allowed to demand all that of *right* belongs to us for paft fervices; this we difclaim. Even the *Spaniards*, who have not thofe fublime ideas of freedom that Englifh men have, are confcious that they have no right to all the fervices of their fellowmen, we mean the *Africans*, whom they have purchafed with their money; therefore they allow them one day in a week to work for themfelve, to enable them to earn money to purchafe the refidue of their time, which they have a right to demand in fuch portions as they are able to pay for (a due appraizment of their fervices being firft made, which always ftands at the purchafe money.) We do not pretend to dictate to you Sir, or to the honorable Affembly, of which you are a member: We acknowledge our obligations to you for what you have already done, but as the people of this province feem to be actuated by the principles of equity and juftice, we cannot but expect your houfe will again take our deplorable cafe into ferious confideration, and give us that ample relief which, *as men*, we have a natural right to.

BUT fince the wife and righteous governor of the univerfe, has permitted our fellow men to make us flaves, we bow in fubmiffion to him, and determine to behave in fuch a manner, as that we may have reafon to expect the divine approbation of, and affiftance in, our peaceable and lawful attempts to gain our freedom.

WE are willing to fubmit to fuch regulations and laws, as may be made relative to us, until we leave the province, which we determine to do as foon as we can from our joynt labours procure money to tranfport ourfelves to fome part of the coaft of *Africa*, where we propofe a fettlement. We are very defirous that you fhould have inftructions relative to us, from your town, therefore we pray you to communicate this letter to them, and afk this favor for us.

In behalf of our fellow flaves in this province,
And by order of their Committee.

PETER BESTES,
SAMBO FREEMAN,
FELIX HOLBROOK,
CHESTER JOIE.

For the REPRESENTATIVE of the town of *Thompson*

Fig. 8: *A committee of slaves circulated this carefully worded request to the Colonial Assembly of Massachusetts in 1773. They applauded the anti-British legislature's "noble stand against the designs of their fellow-men to enslave them" and went on to request their own release from bondage and the chance to return to Africa.*

Work, therefore, dominated the lives of all enslaved African Americans—men and women, young and old. But the nature of that work varied significantly from one place to the next, from one season to the next, and from one generation to the next. Cotton agriculture, though present in Africa, did not yet exist in North America. Later generations of African Americans would be obliged to pick cotton all across the Deep South after 1800, but their ancestors in colonial times faced a very different array of tasks. Most lived in the Chesapeake region and the coastal southeast, where the lengthy growing season promised enormous profits to aggressive white investors once the land had been cleared for plantation agriculture. African newcomers—women as well as men—soon found themselves cutting and burning trees, splitting rails, and building fences. Using an axe and a hatchet, each individual was expected to clear several acres of southern wilderness in a single season.

For some, the work with wood never ended. Buildings were needed, and workers spent long hours felling trees and then squaring the logs with an adze. The huge timbers were placed over saw pits and cut into planks by two men using a two-handled saw. (The person who stood above the beam, known as the "top dog," avoided the shower of sawdust; we still use this phrase for someone in a privileged position.) Guided by an African parent or a white overseer, a skilled black youth might learn to be a wheelwright, a house carpenter, a shingle cutter, a boat builder, or a cabinetmaker. But he was most likely to make barrels, for these huge containers were crucial to the safe shipment of valuable products over long distances. Barrels pieced together from separate staves of wood were needed for fish and rum in New England, for grain and tobacco in the Chesapeake, for rice and indigo in South Carolina. By the 18th century, timber, which had been cleared to make room for plantations, was scarce on Caribbean islands, so staves shaped from American trees were sold to the West Indies, where they were assembled into barrels for shipping Caribbean sugar and molasses.

The transportation needs of the expanding colonies demanded various sorts of labor. Africans found themselves pressed into service building wagons, hammering horseshoes, stitching saddles, and mending harnesses. Amos Fortune, an African who ended his days as a free leatherworker in Jaffrey, New Hampshire, worked for a tanner in Woburn, Massachusetts, for two decades before gaining his freedom. Black South Carolinians built dugout canoes from cypress logs and fashioned larger boats to float the rice crop to Charleston via the winding rivers. After crops were harvested every fall, planters in South Carolina's coastal low country were required to send enslaved workers to dig ditches. Over several generations they created an amazing network of canals—a web of waterways linking local rivers for travel and irrigation. Near Chesapeake Bay, slaves constructed roads along which huge round wooden "hogsheads" of tobacco could be rolled to ships waiting at harbor docks and riverside piers. In Maryland, one of these thoroughfares is still known as "Rolling Road" after more than 200 years.

Sooner or later, all colonial roads led down to the sea and ships. England's North American colonists clustered around rivers and ports. They sold their surplus produce to Europe and received a steady supply of manufactured goods in return— everything from hats and hatchets to china and window glass. They also sent to the West Indies quantities of salt fish, to be used as food for enslaved workers, and supplies of firewood, to be used in boiling sugarcane into molasses. In return, they brought back slaves who had not yet been sold in Caribbean markets, along with barrels of molasses to be made into rum and shipped to Africa as a commodity in the slave trade. In North Carolina, slaves cut pine trees filled with resin and then burned the wood in closed ovens to produce tar and pitch for use by English sailors. French seamen needed similar materials for protecting the hulls and rigging of their ships. In 1724, an English report suggested that rival French colonists in Louisiana were producing pitch and tar and had "already settled four Plantations with fifty Negroes on each to carry on that Work."

Besides working in the dangerous production of tar and pitch, African-American artisans were involved in all aspects of the colonial boat-building trade. Frederick Douglass, at age 11, was sent to work in his master's shipyard near Baltimore in 1829. The young slave's experience, vividly described in his autobiography, must have been shared by generations of African Americans before him.

> It was—"Fred., come help me to cant this timber here." . . . —"Hurra, Fred.! run and bring me a chisel."—"I say, Fred., bear a hand, and get up a fire as quick as lightning under that steam box."—"Halloo, nigger! come, turn this grindstone."—"Come, come! move, move! and bowse this timber forward."—"I say, darky, blast your eyes, why don't you heat up some pitch?"—"Halloo! halloo! halloo!" (Three voices at the same time.) "Come here!—Go there!—Hold on where you are! Damn you, if you move, I'll knock your brains out!" This was my school.

It was one thing to build ships, but quite another to sail on them. Douglass himself recalled how, as a boy growing up near Chesapeake Bay, he used to watch "sails from every quarter of the habitable globe" and wish that he was on board. Numerous colonial slaves, just as ingenious but less well known than Douglass, found ways to leave shore and become harbor pilots and deep-sea sailors. Equiano, for example, was purchased by the captain of a British merchant ship shortly after his arrival in Virginia, and he spent decades sailing the Atlantic, working for different owners on various ships, before finally securing his freedom.

Equiano had never seen the ocean, or even a large river, before being taken from his small village as a boy, but many Africans arrived in America with a knowledge of the sea. Those from coastal regions were experienced swimmers, not as afraid of bathing and diving as most eighteenth-century Europeans. Others were expert fishermen, and they put their skills to good use in the fish-filled bays and rivers of the American coast. Black newcomers in South Carolina and Georgia found an abundance of shrimp (a delicacy well known to many Africans but foreign to Europeans) in the waters surrounding the coastal Sea Islands. They wove casting nets and hauled in schools of tasty shrimp just as they had done in West Africa. In Southern swamps and rivers, the Europeans proved frightened by the strange alligators. Africans, on the other hand, were familiar with killing and eating crocodiles, so many of them knew how to confront such dangerous reptiles without fear.

Black women often worked in the fields, as many of them had done in Africa, but they also assumed primary responsibility for a great deal of domestic labor. House servants were forced to cook and clean, wash and press, sew and mend, to suit the demands of their colonial mistress. With varying degrees of oversight, a plantation cook handled all aspects of food preparation, from tending the garden or visiting the town market to washing the dishes and throwing leftovers to the pigs. Indeed, when it came time to slaughter the hogs and cure their meat, she supervised that complex process as well. Day after day, year after year, she was obliged to balance the endless demands of the white household and the ongoing needs of her own family. Nothing illustrates this conflict more dramatically than the fact that the mother of a black infant was sometimes required to stop suckling her own baby and to serve instead as the wet nurse to a newborn child in the family of her master.

Southern planters noted approvingly that African women were generally experienced agriculturalists, while women coming from Europe usually were not. They also realized that Africans were less troubled by the seasonal bouts of malaria that often sickened European workers (though no one yet understood that a distinctive blood trait now known as sickle cell contributed to this difference). In addition, they observed an obvious benefit in the fact that West Africans were generally familiar with survival in a warm and humid climate. They knew how to take advantage of shade trees and summer breezes in locating their dwellings, and they were familiar with many of the plants and animals that existed in the subtropics.

Where the flora and fauna differed from the Old World, enslaved Africans could turn to local Indians for knowledge. Indian slaves still made up a portion of the colonial work force in the early 18th century. Moreover, Africans were involved in the early Indian wars on the frontier and participated in the extensive fur trade. It was a risky business. The black man who accompanied white trader John Lawson among the Tuscaroras in 1711 was burned at the stake alongside Lawson when hostilities broke out between the Indians and the English. But others survived these encounters and acquired important information, even learning to speak the Indian languages. In 1717, Timboe was one of several enslaved Africans accompanying a large pack train into the Southern backcountry. According to the Commissioners of the Indian Trade, he was "to tend the Pack-Horses" (there were more than twenty) and "to serve as Interpreter."

These frontier activities brought black men into frequent contact with Native Americans, and eventually this aroused the fears of white authorities. They worried about any black person who was carrying a gun, exploring the countryside, and gaining the acquaintance of Indians willing to harbor runaways. Therefore, they passed laws limiting the participation of enslaved Africans in frontier warfare and the Indian trade. They even went so far as to offer handsome rewards to Indians who brought back runaway slaves, dead or alive. By the 1720s, of course, African Americans had already been in contact with Indians for more than 200 years, and this complex and important relationship would continue throughout North America regardless of such laws. Consider the example of Jean Baptiste Point du Sable, who was born in Canada or the Caribbean to a French and an African parent. Little is known about his early life, but by the 1770s, this Afro-French fur trader was living on a 30-acre tract beside Lake Michigan with a Potawatomi Indian woman named Catherine. During the years of the American Revolution, he managed to play off competing British and American interests, emerging after the war as a successful trading post operator. Jean and Catherine raised a son and a daughter, adding 400 acres to their tract and building a log home surrounded by a mill, a bakehouse, a workshop, a smoke house, and barns for the livestock. Their frontier marriage was formally acknowledged with a Catholic wedding service in 1778, but when Catherine died in 1800, Jean sold their extensive property in order to move further west to live with his son in Missouri. The estate proved to be worth $1,200, not including thirty head of cattle, two mules, thirty-eight pigs, and a yard full of chickens. Although du Sable died poor in 1818, the strategic site he had developed would grow to be the vast and booming city of Chicago.

The extent of Indian-African contact in the eighteenth century is evident in the way the Southern diet evolved in colonial times. Such African foods as okra, yams, peanuts, and sesame seeds made their way into Southern cooking. Often they were combined with traditional Indian delicacies, as in gumbo, the famous specialty of Louisiana cuisine. The thick base is made by cooking sliced okra (an African dish) or powdered sassafras (a Choctaw Indian staple) in slowly heated oil. Even the word *gumbo* may come from the Angolan *guingombo* for okra or the Choctaw *kombo ashish* for sassafras powder.

Food containers and utensils also revealed traditions from Africa, reinforced by New World Indian practices. The palmetto tree of coastal Carolina, which appeared strange and exotic to Europeans, was familiar to African newcomers as well as Indian residents. Soon black Carolinians were using strips from the long palmetto leaves to bind together circular baskets of all shapes and sizes, much as they had in Africa. Gourds, like palmetto trees, were familiar to Africans and Indians, as the experience of Esteban in an earlier century made clear. Southern Indians had long used light, durable gourds for bowls, dippers, and storage containers, as had arriving Africans. In contrast, English colonists, coming from a cool climate, had little familiarity with gourds and their practical possibilities. In addition, we now know that African-American artisans were fashioning their own clay pots and bowls, which were different from European earthenware but similar to much Native American pottery. These simple vessels, now known as "colonoware," have been correctly identified only in recent years.

In short, the Africans who survived the Middle Passage brought numerous skills with them and acquired others from Indian neighbors, who already knew which local plants were edible and which had special medicinal value. Ironically, the slaves' ability to persevere and subsist under harsh conditions often benefited their self-styled "owners." Obviously, workers who raised their own food in small garden plots and caught fish in the local stream saved a planter the expense of supplying provisions. A strong man who had hammered iron in Africa needed little instruction in metalworking at a colonial forge. Occasionally Europeans seized and exploited much more than African labor; they took advantage of superior African knowledge as well. The story of profitable rice cultivation in colonial South Carolina is a good example.

After the founding of Carolina in 1670, English colonists spent a full generation seeking a suitable staple crop. In order to have enough food, a few of the earliest enslaved Africans in the settlement began growing rice in the wet swampland, as they had done in their homeland. English planters, who were largely unfamiliar with rice, realized that conditions were excellent for this crop and began to learn more. Production grew rapidly as Africans showed them how to irrigate the plants in the field, pound the rice kernels with a wooden mortar and pestle, and winnow the chaff with a "fanner" basket. Soon slave merchants were advertising workers from the so-called Rice Coast of West Africa, and profits from the sale of Carolina rice were making local plantation owners the richest gentry in North America. French Louisiana began importing Africans aggressively around 1718—the year New Orleans was founded. French officials promptly urged captains to import several Africans "who know how to cultivate rice," along with "hogsheads of rice suitable for planting."

By 1775, roughly half a million African Americans were living and laboring in North America. Throughout the colonies a small proportion were free blacks, but most were legally enslaved, and most lived in the South. As their numbers increased, so did the profits from their work. Wealthy planters acquired more land and bought additional slaves, so an increasing number of enslaved black colonists found themselves working on large plantations. This was especially true in the Chesapeake region, where nearly half of the entire African-American population labored in the tobacco fields of Virginia and Maryland. Thomas Jefferson, still in his early 30s, owned nearly 400 black Virginians on the eve of the Revolution, and George Washington's enslaved labor force was even larger.

Washington, Jefferson, and other members of the Virginia gentry were dismayed to see so much of the wealth generated by their African workers passing into the hands of London merchants instead of into their own pockets. The grievances of white colonists would eventually prompt their demands for freedom from English rule. But eighteenth-century African-Americans gained few rewards from the revolutionary struggle. Nevertheless, black Americans had been engaged in a successful revolutionary battle of their own over several generations. Throughout the 18th century they had been struggling, against tremendous odds, to build the cultural framework that would allow their survival in a harsh and alien land. At times this struggle for survival led individuals and groups to engage in acts of open defiance and revolt. Many lives were lost, but crucial victories were won in gradually laying the foundation for African-American culture. When Thomas Jefferson and George Washington proclaimed the nation's "independence," half a million African Americans remained without their liberty.

CHAPTER 6

Building a Culture

THE GROWING NUMBER of black colonists in America varied dramatically in their backgrounds and experiences. Gambians differed from Angolans, and "saltwater" slaves differed from "country-born." Obvious and important contrasts emerged between field hands and house servants, Northerners and Southerners, town dwellers and rural residents—not to mention the gulf often separating the many who were enslaved from the few who were legally free. Among most of these very different people, however, there began to appear during the 18th century one identifiable African-American culture.

In certain ways, the emergence of African-American culture can be compared with the later appearance of other ethnic cultures in pluralistic America (here *pluralistic* means "composed of many different ethnic groups"). For example, all newcomers—from the earliest African Americans down to the most recent immigrants from Asia, Latin America, the Caribbean, or the Middle East—try to hold on to certain elements of life from their "old country." In addition, all newcomers confront the hard questions posed by American geography. Is the land hotter or colder, wetter or drier, than the home they left behind? How different are the foods and smells, the hills and rivers, the cities and towns? Each group, in short, must adapt to the possibilities and limits of the varied American landscape and climate. Moreover, all new arrivals must confront the world of white, English-speaking Protestants. This portion of the diverse American population gained the upper hand during the colonial era, grew with the country in the nineteenth century, and has dominated the nation's mainstream culture from its beginning.

In other ways, however, the emergence of black culture is unique in American history, for the influx of Africans was *early*, *large*, and *involuntary*. The fact that most Africans, in contrast to other distinctive racial, ethnic, or religious groups, arrived during the eighteenth century means that their roots in America are older and deeper. Black culture has had more than two centuries to influence other parts of the society. Though later migrations to North America have been bigger, none has been so large in comparison to the total American population of the time. Most importantly of all, no other migration to America was involuntary and based entirely upon exploitation. Black immigrants to the strange new land of North America faced lives of physical hardship and constant psychological hurt from one generation to the next. In order to endure in this isolated and confining world of work, it was necessary to forge links that would allow families to form and communities to develop.

Racial slavery as practiced in colonial North America made the creation of stable families extremely hard. Slave captains usually purchased their captives one by one from several African ports. If a husband and wife or mother and daughter somehow managed to stay together and survive until they reached

America, they were likely to be separated at the auction block. Creating new families proved almost as difficult as preserving old ones. Newcomers who overcame the deep sense of grief and loss created by the Middle Passage had to weigh the risk of fresh relationships in the New World. Intimacy was difficult in a realm where neither husbands nor wives controlled their own lives. Either partner could be brutally punished or sold away while the other looked on helplessly; children could be put up for sale and spouses could be raped. White fathers alternately favored and denied their mulatto offspring; free persons of color often lived separately from enslaved relatives. Under such conditions, early African-American family relationships were unstable at best.

Nevertheless, durable families and extensive networks of kinfolk gradually came into being. Masters realized that people with vulnerable and needy loved ones depending on them often proved more obedient and hardworking than single people who lacked local ties. Because it would have limited their power, masters did not recognize legal marriage among slaves, but they encouraged long-term relationships from which they expected to benefit, both through the work of the couple and the labor of their eventual children.

More important than the pressures of the masters were the desires of the people themselves. The harshness and insecurity of their situation increased the need to share the numerous sufferings and rare pleasures with another person. Raising one's own children, even under trying circumstances, could be a greater affirmation than living without children at all. If family members could suddenly be killed or disappear, there was all the more reason to honor each new union, delight in every healthy birth, and extend the network of relations as widely as possible.

Extended slave families reached across generations and linked separate plantations. They were constantly being broken apart and reformed in new ways, adapting to meet the changing and unkind circumstances of plantation life. These emerging family networks played an important role in transmitting cultural patterns and conserving African values. Many slaveowners welcomed these ties as a way to limit black independence, but family bonds were not always such a conservative force for preserving the slavery system as most masters thought. After all, families fostered loyalty and trust; they conveyed information and belief; and they provided a strong shelter within which to hide and a reliable launching pad from which to venture forth.

By providing much-needed solace and support, the positive ties of family gave encouragement to individuals and groups who were coming together, against formidable odds, to forge the beginnings of a common culture. Slowly, over the course of the 18th century, these exploited Americans discovered the means for their own survival. They called upon their African past as well as their immediate surroundings; they borrowed from the European and Native American cultures they encountered, and drew strength and support from one another. Gradually, over time, they built a unique and varied way of life that was their own and that gave them the faith to carry on.

Music undoubtedly provided one crucial starting point for this complex process of cultural building. Certainly no element was more central, or illustrates the process more clearly. Recognizable African harmonies, intonations, and rhythms sounded familiar to strangers from different regions who could not converse with one another. This shared musical background drew together people who still spoke different languages. Songs of grief, worship, love, and work could reassure listeners even before they discovered other common ground. A musical tradition that stressed improvisation provided a welcome hearth where the sharing process could begin. Eventually, a similar sharing process would touch almost every aspect of cultural life, but for many the earliest common links were through music.

Drums, universal among African societies, served as one common denominator, and different styles of drumming and diverse ways of making drums were soon shared. Moreover, this kind of exchange through an emphasis on percussion instruments reached beyond diverse Africans. Native Americans found that the use of drums and rattles represented one of many cultural elements they shared with people from sub-Saharan Africa. Europeans, startled by the extent of African drumming and fearful that this skill sometimes provided a secret means of communication, outlawed the use of drums by slaves in various colonies. South Carolina's strict Negro Code of 1740 prohibited slaves from "using or keeping drums, horns, or other loud instruments, which may call together, or give sign or notice to one another of their wicked designs and purposes."

Such fears did not prevent white colonists from recruiting free blacks to serve as military musicians (as they were already doing in England). Virginia's Militia Act of 1723 allowed that "Such free Negroes, Mulattos or Indians, as are capable, may be listed and emploied as Drummers or Trumpeters." Several generations later such a black drummer, Mat Anderson, often visited the kitchen of Thomas Jefferson. When he would set down his huge drum, Isaac, a slave boy in Jefferson's household, "would beat on it & Mat larnt him how to beat." A fellow slave recalled that Isaac (only six years old) was "big enough to beat the drum, but couldn't raise it off the ground; would hold it tilted over to one side and beat on it that way." Similarly, in Charleston in 1767,

twelve-year-old John Marrant joined older musicians who assembled to practice and teach in the evenings. "Here my improve-
ment was so rapid," he later recalled, "that in a twelve-month's
time I became master of both the violin and the French horn."

Learning to play European instruments allowed a black person to gain status in the community, avoid harsh tasks, and travel
widely. Notices in colonial newspapers suggest such slave musicians were in constant demand. The Boston *Evening Post* advertised a man who "plays well upon a *flute*, and not so well upon a
violin." Similarly, the *Virginia Gazette* commented upon one
musician: "He is a Native of *Africa*, speaks *English* tolerably, and
plays on the *French* horn." In 1768, the same newspaper
described another man, born in Virginia, as follows: "He makes
fiddles, and can play the fiddle, and work at the carpenters trade."

For each person who learned to make and play European
instruments, there were many others who recalled how to make
and play African instruments. Besides manufacturing a variety
of drums, African Americans also re-created various string and
percussion instruments used on the other side of the Atlantic.
The most popular import was the banjo (often called a bandore,
banjer, or banjar). "The instrument proper to them is the
Banjar," wrote Thomas Jefferson, "which they brought hither
from Africa." "I well remember," recalled another writer,

> that in Virginia and Maryland the favourite and almost only instru-
> ment in use among the slaves there was a *bandore*; or, as they
> pronounced the word, *banjer*. Its body was a large hollow gourd,
> with a long handle attached to it, strung with catgut, and played on
> with the fingers. . . . My memory supplies me with a couplet of one
> of their songs . . . :
> Negro Sambo play fine *banjer*,
> Make his fingers go like handsaw.

When William Smith visited West Africa as a surveyor for Britain's Royal Africa Company in the 1720s, he described the xylophone known as a balafo (also ballafoe, barrafou, or barrafoo) and later published a picture of it. The instrument consisted of 11 thin planks of differing lengths, supported over large gourd resonators of various sizes. White schoolmaster John Harrower told of seeing a similar instrument when he visited a fellow teacher on a Virginia plantation in 1775. "I spent the afternoon in conversation & hearing him play the Fiddle. He also made a Niger come & play on an Instrument call'd a Barrafou. The body of it is an oblong box with the mouth up & stands on four sticks put in bottom, & cross the [top] is laid 11 lose sticks upon [which] he beats." The music of this unusual instrument was well known locally, as suggested by a sarcastic comment in the *Virginia Gazette* the following year, when many blacks were joining the British rather than supporting their masters' push for independence. With obvious irritation, the editor observed that these people expected to "be gratified with the use of the sprightly and enlivening *barrafoo*" behind British lines, rather than being stirred by "the drowsy fife and drum" of the patriot cause.

The pattern is clear. Black colonists learned from one another and from non-Africans as well. They recalled old songs and sounds and instruments, and they borrowed new ones. Over several generations, they gave birth to a fresh and changing musical tradition. They drew heavily upon their varied Old World heritage, but they also built, necessarily, on the novel influences and sorrowful circumstances of their strange new land. The result was a range of musical expression that was both African and American. It varied widely in its forms from New Orleans to Philadelphia, or from a Georgia slave cabin to a

Boston kitchen. But it contained unifying threads that became stronger over time. After 1800 this consolidation would become clearer still, as access to African roots diminished, communication among black Americans increased, and full entry into the dominant culture remained off limits.

The same conditions applied to much more than music. All elements of life in the strange new land seemed to depend upon involvement with other Africans and with non-Africans as well. Language provides a dramatic case in point. Even before they reached America, enslaved Africans began to learn words and phrases from one another. Shipmates from the same area often found they could comprehend portions of their neighbors' languages. Equiano remembered his amazement—standing on a dock in Barbados, after surviving the Atlantic crossing—when he saw horses for the first time in his life. "While I was in this astonishment," he recalled, "one of my fellow prisoners spoke to a countryman of his, about the horses, who said they were the same kind they had in their country. I understood them, though they were from a distant part of Africa."

In the New World, black newcomers were soon forced to assimilate at least one European language—whether English, French, German, Dutch, Spanish, or Portuguese—and often learned more than one. Among runaways advertised in the *Pennsylvania Gazette* during the 1750s, those who could speak several European tongues included a shoemaker and fiddler named Tom (age thirty-seven), "a labouring man" named Will (age twenty-nine) whose mother was an Indian, and a mulatto named Harry (age twenty-five) who grew up in Virginia and "chews Tobacco much." Likewise, Bevis, who ran away in 1766, was described as "a smart lively Fellow, and . . . a midling Scholar" in his thirties who "talks very good English and

Dutch." Persons who had a Native American parent, or a job on the frontier, or who had lived in a tribal village, might have spoken an Indian language as well. Musician John Marrant, for instance, resided for several years among the Cherokees and learned to converse with them.

Our own experiences today can tell us a good deal about this process of living in several cultures at the same time. Suppose a fourteen-year-old girl arrives at the local public school from abroad. Students and teachers might ask: How old was she when she left her homeland? How many other people from her country or continent now live in her immediate neighborhood? How much daily contact does she have with English speakers and with non-English speakers? The answers could tell a good deal about her life, and these same questions would apply to a fourteen-year-old African girl in colonial times. If she lived on a large plantation in South Carolina, where blacks were in a majority and contact with whites was limited, she might speak "Gullah," a complex blend of African languages and English. But if she lived in a white household in New England she would learn the English of that region. This was the case for Phillis Wheatley, an African girl carried to Boston in 1761 at age seven, who published her first poem in English eight years later.

Certain African words were especially likely to survive. Some, for example, were common to numerous African tongues, such as *Cudjo*, the day name for a boy born on Monday. Others happened to coincide closely in sound with a English word. An African girl born on Thursday and given the traditional day name *Abba* become known in America as *Abby*. A few terms overlapped in both sound and meaning and therefore had a strong chance of survival. In the Mende language of West Africa, *sasi* could mean "a prideful boaster," or "to ridicule contemptuously." In the Gullah speech of the South Carolina low country, therefore, *sasi* continued to mean "proud one" or "to ridicule," but this matched so closely the common English term "saucy" that it probably reinforced the use of "sassy" and "to sass" in American English. Other words endured simply because they were used so often. In the Congo region, *tota* means "to pick up," and enslavement involved so much lifting and carrying that "to tote" became a universal Southern term.

The same factors that shaped how newcomers might speak also determined other aspects of life. The clothes they wore and the homes they built, how they styled their hair and cooked their food—all these things were influenced by many forces, even in the confining world of enslavement. Obviously one powerful force—though not always the most important one— was the rule of the masters. Colonial assemblies passed laws defining the cheap fabrics suitable for slave clothing and forbidding fancier apparel. But appearance was difficult to legislate. When Peter Deadfoot ran away in Virginia in 1768, his master advertised that this versatile man (a shoemaker, butcher, plowman, sawyer, boatman, and "one of the best scythemen . . . in America") was also "extremely fond of dress." Similarly, when a "Guiney Country" slave named Erskyne disappeared in South Carolina in 1773, his owner protested haughtily that he had taken clothes which were "really too good for any of his Colour."

On certain holidays, colonial blacks were allowed to dress in extravagant English finery. By the 1770s, for instance, a tradition of black celebrations had grown up around the annual white election day in such New England towns as Newport, Rhode Island; Hartford, Connecticut; and Salem, Massachusetts. Once a year, during these sanctioned "Negro Election Days," elegantly dressed black "kings" and "governors" borrowed fine horses, large hats, or dress swords from the whites who endorsed the entertainment. On other special occasions, particularly in the South, blacks often chose to dress in styles and colors and materials that invoked their free African past. By the nineteenth century, and perhaps even earlier on some plantations, slaves in certain localities were dressing in African costumes and dancing to African rhythms during the event that would become known as Jonkonnu. These festivities usually occurred during the Christmas season, and the lead dancer often wore an elaborate mask or headdress and had colorful rags and ribbons swirling from his costume.

Like clothing, hairstyles also represented a complex area for cultural negotiation. Some black men became barbers for whites, learning to cut the hair and powder the wigs of their master; some black women attended to the hair of their mistress and her children, according to the latest European fashions. But how African Americans wore their own hair depended upon the individual's preference, an owner's rules, and the limits of time. For girls to braid their hair in elaborate cornrows—then as now—was satisfying and attractive, but also very time-consuming. For men to tease their hair into swelling "Afros" drew comments—and even punishments—from white masters who were often offended by such "foreign" styles. Hats and bonnets, bandannas and braids often provided varied and colorful compromises in the realm of hairdressing.

In some areas, necessity may have agreed with preference. Many early slave cabins, for example, had dirt floors and yards without grass. Did this represent simply an unwillingness of the planter to provide boards for floors and seeds for grass? Probably not, for many blacks preferred the African tradition of a clay floor, pounded hard and kept clean, just as they valued a carefully swept yard, even though these practices demanded considerable work. Similarly, the thatching of houses with palmetto leaves and the weaving of baskets with coils of sweet grass represent cherished traditions remembered from Africa and practiced in America. What are we to make of the presence of simple handmade pottery (called colonoware, because it originated in the colonial era) at eighteenth-century slave sites across the South? Though iron cooking pots and cracked dishes and pitchers from the big house are also evident, archaeologists now believe many African Americans may have preferred to fashion their own bowls for cooking in a more traditional way.

Finally, consider how these early African Americans fashioned the mental and moral aspects of their emerging culture. In short, what did they think and believe? The question is challenging, and the full answer remains to be found. But in the realm of ideas, as in the material domain, their lives seem to have been varied and creative, despite overwhelming constraints. At the center of black thought throughout the 18th century, a crucial debate was occurring over the acceptance of European Christianity. Many "saltwater slaves"—including some, like Job ben Solomon, who had been raised in the Muslim faith—held firmly to their African religious beliefs. A white missionary in South Carolina recalled the answer of one elderly African when asked why he refused to take part in the rituals of the Church of England. The old man replied simply, "I prefer to live by that which I remember."

On the other hand, certain slaves who had left Africa at an early age or had been born in the New World accepted the Protestant Christian faith of the whites around them, as did young Phillis Wheatley in Boston. In an early poem she wrote:

'Twas mercy brought me from my Pagan land,
Taught my benighted soul to understand
That there's a God, that there's a Saviour too:
Once I redemption neither sought nor knew.

But most African Americans fell somewhere in the middle. Torn between the remembered belief systems of their ancestors and the dominant religion of their masters, they combined these two worlds in a process of evolution that took many generations.

Over time, white masters increasingly demanded, and even rewarded, an outward profession of Christianity among many second- and third-generation African Americans. But they had little control over the forms that religion might take, and black colonists, slave and free, gradually began to shape a faith that gave special meaning to traditional Protestant beliefs. Black Christians favored music and song; they emphasized baptism and down-to-earth preaching. Denied the right to read, they stressed Old Testament stories that suited their situation, such as the Hebrew captivity in Egypt. Most of all, they considered carefully the New Testament portrait of Jesus Christ as a friend of the afflicted and a redeemer of the weak. We know that George Liele, the slave of a Baptist deacon in Burke County, Georgia, used to preach to fellow slaves on the text: "Come unto me all ye that labour, and are heavy laden, and I will give you rest."

By the mid eighteenth century—during a period of revitalized Protestant zeal among whites known as the Great Awakening—a minority of black Americans were beginning to embrace Christianity. Black preachers appeared as early as 1743, and by the mid-1770s, George Liele and a small group of converted slaves along the Savannah River established the Silver Bluff Baptist Church, the first black Protestant church in

America. Under the influence of both white and black itinerant Methodist and Baptist ministers, the number of African-American converts would grow during the next generation. But even those who accepted Christianity retained certain African spirit beliefs and burial customs that would become vital aspects of the emerging African-American culture.

CHAPTER 7

Breaking the Bonds

CHALLENGING ARBITRARY rule is the world's most difficult task, especially when undemocratic control has become firmly established. Faced with overwhelming odds, many in bondage elect survival over open resistance, and their choice is as logical and understandable as it is painful. For those who choose to defy the odds and test the boundaries of their confinement, no one effective model exists. Therefore, they try all imaginable modes of resistance: calculated and spontaneous, covert and direct, psychological and physical, individual and collective. Despite the monotony of enslavement, no two circumstances are ever exactly alike, so the best tactic yesterday may be the most costly or foolhardy today. Adaptability is crucial, and bravery is a constant ingredient, for even the smallest gesture of defiance can result in cruel punishment and lasting consequences.

Small acts of resistance, though dangerous, were regular events in the house of bondage. The slightest command could be wrongly interpreted or carelessly carried out. The easiest task could be purposely bungled or endlessly extended. By breaking a tool or pretending to be sick, slaves could avoid a whole day's work, gaining needed rest for themselves and undercutting steady profits for their owner. Workers forced to labor to support the life of a master often felt justified in appropriating some of the food they had grown and prepared, even if the planter viewed this activity as stealing. Elaborate trading and marketing networks grew up to exchange such goods. Though the owner might encourage slave gardens to reduce his own expense in feeding his work force, he objected when these gardens received more attention than his fields or when the slaves sold their own produce and defiantly pocketed the profits.

No act of defiance was more commonplace than running away. Even brief departures could provide relief from an oppressive overseer. But such disappearances also deprived the owners of their daily profits, so penalties were often harsh, especially for repeat offenders. In May 1748, twenty-year-old Cato was wearing more than a flannel jacket, worn leather breeches, tattered shoes, and an old beaver hat when he slipped away once again from the silversmith shop of his Philadelphia owner. According to the *Pennsylvania Gazette*, he had been forced to wear "irons on his legs, and about his neck," though the paper added that he "probably has cut them off, as he has done several times before on the like occasion." When Hannah, age 18, ran away from her Virginia master six times in as many months, she had her hair cut "in a very irregular Manner, as a Punishment for offences." In North Carolina, individuals who persisted in running away were often forced to wear heavy neck-yokes as a penalty.

Magistrates could not assess fines against persons who were forbidden to own property. Therefore, minor acts of defiance prompted harsh physical punishment, such as whipping, branding, or the wearing of shackles. Moreover, masters were free to inflict their own forms of retribution. Equiano never forgot the horrible sight that confronted him the first time he entered a white dwelling, just days after he had arrived in Virginia:

> I had seen a black woman slave as I came through the house, who was cooking the dinner, and the poor creature was cruelly loaded with various kinds of iron machines; she had one particularly on her head, which locked her mouth so fast that she could scarcely speak; and could not eat nor drink. I was much astonished and shocked at this contrivance, which I afterwards learned was called the iron muzzle.

Seeing or experiencing such inhuman treatment could only sharpen the resentments and deepen the bitterness of a worker in bondage. The resulting rage often found expression in acts of extreme violence. Overseers were beaten to death by angry workhands in the fields; masters and their families were poisoned by desperate servants in the kitchen. Setting fires also became a favored act of defiance, since arson, like poisoning food, was difficult to prove and easy to deny. Burning a loaded barn at harvest time was a way to avoid unwelcome work and deprive the owner of a year's profits. Even the desperate act of suicide took on a double meaning, for it freed the black worker from bondage and deprived the white owner of a valuable investment.

Black violence against the system of slavery ranged from spontaneous individual acts to elaborate conspiracies involving numerous people. Among enslaved African Americans, as among any people living under totalitarian control, thought of rebellion was universal; open talk of such matters was far more guarded; and the undertaking itself was the bold and rare exception, for a variety of reasons. Urban slaves were closely watched, and rural slaves were widely dispersed; organized patrols were commonplace, and informants were everywhere. Long working hours and wide distances made communication difficult, as did forced illiteracy and diverse ethnic backgrounds. Despite such huge obstacles, brave individuals joined in risky coalitions to attempt mass escape or armed insurrection.

Leaders of such collective designs always had to consider the same array of difficult questions. Could they build wide support without opening the door to dissention or betrayal? Could they take advantage of divisions among whites, or natural disasters such as storms or epidemics, without sacrificing control over timing? Could they make, buy, steal, or capture enough weapons to win an immediate victory that would bring additional people and resources to their cause? Could they generate the ruthless violence needed for such an undertaking, while still enforcing the restraint and cooperation necessary for success? Could they learn from earlier experience without becoming too discouraged by the woeful outcome of past conspiracies? Often, the answer to several of these questions was "no," and the plotters reluctantly dropped their scheme before passing the point of no return.

Occasionally, however, an event took on a life of its own, as rumors of revolt fueled fears among whites and raised hopes among African Americans. Word of a foreign war, a heavenly sign, or a slave rebellion in some other colony could quickly bring matters to a head, increasing the sense of urgency among enslaved blacks and the feelings of paranoia among those who exploited them. In New York City, in 1712, workers desiring

their freedom set fire to a building and attacked those summoned to put out the blaze. They managed to kill nine persons
and wound seven others, but they failed to spark a larger revolt.
Half a dozen accused conspirators committed suicide after their
capture, and more than twenty were put to death, some by being
burned alive. According to New York's governor, "There has
been the most exemplary punishment that could possibly be
thought of."

Capital punishment was also used in the small French colony
of Louisiana, when several hundred Bambara people, who had
recently been brought from Africa, planned a revolt that was to
begin in late June 1731. The rebellion might have succeeded,
but a remark by a defiant African woman tipped off authorities.
They were surprised to learn that the leader was a man known
as Samba Bambara, who had worked as an interpreter for the
slave traders at Galam on the Senegal River in West Africa.
After falling out of favor with French authorities there, he had
been thrown aboard the slave ship *Annibal* in 1726 and shipped
to Louisiana, where he was soon put to work as a trusted overseer. According to Le Page du Pratz, who investigated the case,
eight suspected leaders, including Samba, were "clapt in irons"
by authorities and then "were put to the torture of burning
matches; which, though several times repeated, could not bring
them to make any confession." When further evidence prompted an admission of guilt, du Pratz reported that "the eight
Negroes were condemned to be broken alive on the wheel"—
tied to a wagon wheel and battered severely until they gradually died of shock. Meanwhile, the woman who had revealed the
plot was sentenced "to be hanged before their eyes; which was

accordingly done." Even then, rumors of revolt continued, but an uprising predicted to begin during midnight mass on Christmas 1731 never materialized.

Meanwhile, slaves had been escaping occasionally from South Carolina and making their way to St. Augustine in northeast Florida. Spanish officials had bestowed freedom on some of the refugees, in hopes of disrupting the neighboring English colony, while others, such as a Mandingo man named Francisco Menendez, were resold into servitude. In 1728, Menendez was made captain of the slave militia, a unit organized to help protect St. Augustine from English attack. In 1733, the Spanish king issued an edict granting freedom to runaway slaves reaching St. Augustine, and in 1738, the local governor granted these newcomers a town site several miles north of the port city. In return, dozens of converted freedmen pledged to shed their "last drop of blood in defense of the Great Crown of Spain and the Holy Faith, and to be the most cruel enemies of the English." With Menendez as their leader, they constructed a fortification known as Mose (or Moosa or Mosa). Two decades later, this small fort (which has recently been located and excavated) still sheltered a community of sixty-seven men, women, and children.

By 1739, a great many of the 40,000 African Americans in bondage in South Carolina were aware that the Spaniards in Florida had offered freedom to slaves from English colonies. In September, when word reached Charleston of the outbreak of open war between England and Spain, the news helped trigger an uprising at Stono Landing south of the city. During the brief and bloody Stono Rebellion, scores of slaves killed their English masters and began marching toward Fort Mose and Spanish St. Augustine, only to be intercepted before their numbers could swell. Fearful of the colony's expanding black majority, officials displayed the heads of executed rebels on poles to discourage future revolts. In addition, they placed a prohibitive duty, or tax, on slaves imported from abroad for several years, and they passed a new Negro Act further restricting the movement and assembly of black South Carolinians. A suspected slave plot in New York in 1741 led to even more fearsome reprisals, fueled by suggestions of underground support and encouragement from Spanish Jesuits and local poor whites.

British conflict with Spain had given hope to slaves in England's North American colonies. Similarly, when England and France became locked in an all-out imperial war in the 1750s, white colonists again became anxious. They feared that enslaved African Americans would take advantage of warfare on the frontiers and seek to challenge their miserable condition. In 1755, British troops under General Edward Braddock suffered a shocking defeat in the backcountry at the hands of the French and their Indian allies. When word of the setback at Fort Duquesne reached the governor of Maryland, he immediately circulated a notice that slaves should be "well observed & watched," and he ordered the colony's militia units "to be prepared to quell it in case any Insurrection should be occasioned by this Stroke."

Officials in Virginia also worried about the potential for rebellion. More than 100,000 blacks now made up well over a third of the total population in that province, and many of the white militiamen were absent in the war. The lieutenant governor reported that local slaves had become "very audacious" in the wake of Braddock's defeat in the Ohio Valley. "These poor Creatures imagine," he wrote condescendingly, that the French "will give them their Freedom. We have too many here, but I hope we shall be able to defeat the Designs of our Enemies and keep these Slaves in proper Subject'n." In South Carolina, where blacks outnumbered whites by roughly three to two, authorities made plans to separate Charleston from the mainland with a canal (to be dug by slaves), so the city might be somewhat "protected against an Insurrection of the Negroes" in the surrounding countryside or an attack by Indians from the frontier.

Charleston's leaders were not wrong to think that their town and their lives were in serious danger. In March 1759, with warfare again brewing on the South Carolina frontier, a free black man named Philip John was whipped and branded for spreading talk of insurrection and saying that within six months all the whites "would be killed." Enraged rather than deterred by his harsh punishment, John expanded his design throughout the spring. He traveled through the country, claiming to have had a vision that in September (the month of the earlier rebellion at Stono) "the Sword shou'd go thru' the Land." After this bloody revolution, he argued, "there should be no more White King's Governor or great men, but the Negroes should live happily and have Laws of their own." When Charleston officials got wind of the cabal, they arrested Philip John once again. They soon reported that he and his associates apparently had planned to seize a storehouse filled with arms and ammunition, "and then with what force they could collect to have marched to this town." For his dream of revolt, John was put to death.

The end of the great war of empire brought dramatic changes to the colonies. In Paris in 1762, British representatives sat down with envoys from France and Spain to negotiate a final peace. Their treaty, completed the following year, gave decisive advantages to the victorious British under their young monarch,

George III. From the king of France, they received control over Canada. From Spain, the Catholic ally of France, they gained hold of what had for 200 years been Spanish Florida. These sweeping shifts in the colonial landscape had an immediate impact on all the peoples of eastern North America. Among Indians, for example, it is no coincidence that a major uprising known as Pontiac's Rebellion began in 1763, as Native Americans in the Great Lakes region lost their strategic bargaining position between French and English colonizers.

Many African Americans also felt an immediate impact from the peace settlement. In Florida, hundreds of blacks had been imported as laborers from the West Indies or had escaped from slavery in the neighboring English colonies. Most of them departed with the Spanish as they evacuated St. Augustine in 1763. At the same time, thousands of African Americans enslaved in nearby Georgia and South Carolina saw a sudden end to their dream of escaping to Fort Mose, as the freedom fighters of the Stono Rebellion had attempted to do a generation earlier. Florida quickly changed from an outpost of possible black liberty to a new frontier for English plantations. Rich investors in Charleston and Savannah transported several thousand workers to British Florida in hopes of earning quick profits from slave labor. A few of these African Americans managed to escape and join bands of Creek Indians in what would soon be known as the Seminole nation. The rest died in bondage.

Elsewhere on the British colonial frontier, the end of the so-called French and Indian War also brought immediate change for African Americans. In the North, numerous servants and free blacks had taken advantage of the turmoil of war to travel more freely. Some served white officers, while others cut roads, built fortifications, and transported supplies. Still others enlisted as soldiers. Garshom Prince, for example, had been born in New England in 1733 and apparently went to war with Captain Robert Durkee. He must have been issued a musket to fight, for he inscribed a traditional powder container made from a cow's horn, when the soldiers paused at Crown Point in 1761 following their victory over the French. Seventeen years later, at age forty-five, Prince was back in service in the American Revolution, fighting for the patriot side. When he was killed in the Battle of Wyoming, Pennsylvania, in 1778, he was once again carrying his carved powder horn. The years between the end of one great war and the beginning of another would be eventful ones for African Americans in their strange new land.

To the west of the English colonies, the end of the war with France also brought change for African Americans. George III and his government ministers were fearful that expanding settlement would encroach on Native American lands and provoke an expensive Indian war. Britain, deeply in debt after the struggle with France, wanted to avoid such a costly undertaking. So the king proclaimed a boundary line running along the top of the Appalachian mountains to divide the Atlantic colonies from Indian nations living in the Ohio and Mississippi river valleys. This so-called Proclamation Line, plus the willingness of colonial officials to pay bounties to Native Americans for capturing runaways, held down the number of enslaved blacks who risked seeking freedom in Indian country. An act by the Virginia Assembly "thought it good Policy . . . to keep up and increase that natural aversion which happily subsists between Negroes and Indians."

Efforts to prohibit interracial mixing on the frontier were not new. When a German named Christian Priber had gone to live among the Cherokees in the 1730s, announcing his plans for an interracial utopia without private property where all races would be welcome, he was hunted down by authorities and imprisoned in Georgia until he died in 1744. Nevertheless, the backcountry was so large and so thinly populated that it was impossible for white authorities to prevent nonwhites from settling together along the frontier. In 1740, Molly Barber, daughter of a wealthy white New England family, eloped with James Chaugham, a Narragansett Indian. The couple established the small community of Barkhamsted in northwest Connecticut, which soon drew a number of Indians, poor whites, and free blacks. In 1758, Mary Jamison, a Scots-Irish immigrant girl, was captured by Indians and lived most of her life among the Senecas in what is now upstate New York. She later told of staying briefly with two African-American runaways at their remote cabin near the Genesee River. She and her children helped harvest their corn crop and passed the winter in their frontier homestead.

Besides affecting African Americans on the borders of the empire, Britain's dramatic triumph over France also had a swift impact upon blacks living in the heart of the mainland colonies. Soon after 1763, the political climate began to change dramatically.

CHAPTER 8

"Liberty! Liberty!"

ENGLAND'S WAR with France had been a long and expensive struggle; it had taken place on land and sea, and it had extended to several continents. As a result, the British crown had built up an enormous public debt. Therefore, no sooner had victory celebrations ended than the government in London began pressing for new taxes to replenish empty coffers. With residents of England already heavily taxed, Parliament turned its attention to the colonies. Their economies had grown and prospered under the protection of the British crown and had benefited directly from the recent war. In the past, England had asked its colonists to pay only duties designed to regulate trade. Now, however, officials suggested that perhaps it was time to levy taxes to raise revenues, even if the colonists were not directly represented in the English Parliament.

In 1765, Parliament approved the controversial Stamp Act, taxing the colonists by obliging them to purchase a government stamp for such simple transactions as buying a newspaper, filing a will, or selling a piece of property. Extensive protests forced the law to be repealed, but it was followed by other revenue measures that intensified debate. British soldiers and sailors used to maintain order became objects of scorn, and the king's troops were frequently attacked. When Parliament passed the Tea Act in 1773, suspicious local leaders saw the offer of cheap tea as a device to trick the colonies into accepting the principle of taxation by Parliament. Colonists vowed not to purchase English tea and even threw boxes of tea into Boston harbor. In 1774, an irate Parliament responded with a series of "Coercive Acts," prompting colonial leaders to organize a Continental Congress that would work out the American response to the intrusive British legislation. British troops met armed resistance when they attempted to secure government powder supplies in Lexington, Massachusetts, in April 1775, and in July 1776, the Continental Congress voted to declare independence from Great Britain.

As participants or observers, African Americans were close to all these important events leading up to the American Revolution. They witnessed firsthand the mounting pressures for an armed revolt against the strongest empire on earth. During a Stamp Act protest in Wilmington, North Carolina, for example, the royal governor sent food and drink in an effort to placate white demonstrators. Not willing to be bought off, the crowd "immediately broke in the heads of the Barrels of Punch and let it run into the street." According to a firsthand account, they refused to roast the ox offered to them by the governor. Instead, they put its head on display "in the Pillory and gave the Carcass to the Negroes" who were looking on. Equiano was working as a slave on a small vessel in the

Caribbean when word reached America that such protests had brought an end to the Stamp Act. He recalled sailing into Charleston harbor at night and seeing "the town illuminated; the guns were fired, and bonfires and other demonstrations of joy shown, on account of repeal of the stamp act."

Crispus Attucks, son of a black man and an Indian woman, played a central role in the Boston Massacre of 1770, in which British redcoats killed five colonists. Described as "6 Feet two Inches high" with "short curl'd hair," Attucks had run away from his master in Framingham, Massachusetts, in 1750. Twenty years later, at age forty-seven, he was working as a sailor out of the Bahamas, aboard a boat bound from Boston to North Carolina. On the evening of March 5, 1770, Attucks played a leading part in the bloody skirmish on King Street. When attorney John Adams (later the second president of the United States) defended the British soldiers at their trial, he argued they had been provoked by a "mob" made up of "a motley rabble of saucy boys, negroes and mulattoes, Irish teagues [slang for Irishmen] and outlandish jack tarrs [sailors from foreign ports]." "Attucks," he told the court, "appears to have undertaken to be the hero of the night, and to lead this army with banners, to form them in the first place in Dock square, and march them up to King street with their clubs."

Andrew, a slave witness who testified at the same trial, recalled seeing Attucks and his band arrive on the scene, where a bitter scuffle was already in progress. The new contingent was shouting loudly and crying, "Damn them, they dare not fire, we are not afraid of them." According to Andrew, "One of these people, a stout man with a long cordwood stick," whom he later identified as Attucks, "threw himself in, and made a blow at the officer," crying out, "kill the dogs, knock them over." Similarly,

John Adams argued that the "stout Molatto fellow" waded into the fray "and with one hand took hold of a bayonet, and with the other knocked the man down." Attucks's actions cost him his life. According to published accounts, he was the first to fall—"killed on the Spot, two Balls entering his Breast." When Boston staged an elaborate public funeral for the martyrs killed in this clash, "all the Bells tolled in solemn Peal" throughout the town. In subsequent years, colonial radicals invoked the name of Crispus Attucks as the first person who had given his life for the patriot cause.

Other African Americans would risk their lives, even before the Declaration of Independence. When Paul Revere summoned the Minutemen to oppose British troops at Concord and Lexington in April 1775, a number of black men living in Massachusetts responded to the call. They included Cato Stedman, Cuff Whitemore, and Cato Boardman from Cambridge; Job Potama and Isaiah Bayoman from Stoneham; Peter Salem from Braintree; Prince Easterbrooks from Lexington, Pompy from Brookline; and David Lamson, an elderly mulatto who had fought in the French and Indian War. Later that same year, at the Battle of Bunker Hill, Cuff Whitemore and Peter Salem again saw action, along with nearly twenty other African Americans. Salem Poor, a black freeman from Andover, fought so bravely that some of his white colleagues later petitioned that this "Brave & gallent Soldier" deserved a reward, since he had "behaved like an Experienced officer" throughout the conflict.

Crispus Attucks has become a remembered figure in American history, and a picture of Peter Salem at Bunker Hill has appeared on a U.S. postage stamp. But there are other black men and women from the decade before the revolution who are less well known and who deserve greater recognition. Individually and collectively, they were involved in their own struggle for liberty. They faced tremendous odds and they took enormous risks. Loyal to the principle of freedom, they listened to the competing rhetoric of white patriots and the British crown. Would either side in the mounting debate include African Americans as free and equal members of society? Unfortunately, the response turned out to be "no." But during the decade before 1776 (and the decade after as well) this fateful answer remained uncertain.

After all, there were moral and logical arguments why Englishmen on one or both sides of the Atlantic might finally decide to renounce race slavery. For one thing, a few whites, led by pioneering Quakers such as John Woolman and Anthony Benezet, were showing an interest in abolishing the institution of slavery—an idea that enslaved African Americans had supported unanimously for more than a century. Not only were notions of human equality beginning to gain favor, but politicians and strategists on both sides of the Atlantic were anxious to appear consistent in arguing over "British liberties." White colonists who claimed they were being "enslaved" by British tyranny were frequently reminded of their hypocrisy. How could they pretend to be "advocates for the liberties of mankind," one critic asked, when they were "trampling on the sacred natural rights and privileges of Africans" at the same moment? How indeed, wondered Abigail Adams in Boston. She reminded her husband, John Adams, that white colonists were preparing to fight for the same liberty that "we are daily robbing and plundering from those who have as good a right to freedom as we have."

Black colonists were ready to fight for their own freedom. They knew they might gain from any dissent that divided the whites who dominated their lives. In Charleston in October 1765, white demonstrators calling themselves the Sons of Liberty took to the streets to oppose the Stamp Act. They chanted "Liberty! Liberty!" and displayed banners reading "Liberty and no Stamp Act." They even paraded through town with a British flag upon which they had written the word *LIBERTY*. A local grand jury protested that slaves, encouraged by such actions, were soon taking to the streets "at all times in the night" and gathering in large numbers on Sundays, much to the distress of whites. When the wife of a merchant overheard two slaves discussing a possible uprising on the night before Christmas, authorities took steps to prevent the usual "Firing Guns by way of rejoycing on Christmas Eve." Though armed guards patrolled day and night for weeks, one planter reported that this did not prevent some brave African Americans from shouting out in public for "Liberty."

Even distant events could provide rays of hope. In 1772, a judge in London ruled, in the well-publicized case of a slave named Somerset, that it was illegal to hold anyone in bondage in England, regardless of race. When word of this stunning decision reached the southern colonies, it created a predictable stir among enslaved workers. Virginia newspapers soon carried ads for black runaways who had disappeared in hopes of securing passage to England. Bacchus, for example, had headed for the coast "to board a vessel for Great Britain," according to his owner, due to "the knowledge he had . . . of Somerset's Case." Phillis Wheatley spoke for all blacks in 1774 when she observed that God had placed a "love of freedom" and a dislike "of

Oppression" in "every human Breast. We Africans, though enslaved, are no different," the young writer asserted; "the same Principle lives in us."

These were not empty words. The previous year, four slaves in Boston seeking independence for blacks in Massachusetts had petitioned the colonial legislature. Whether out of irony or flattery, they began by stating: "We expect great things from men who have made such a noble stand against the designs of their *fellow-men* to enslave them." They asked for the right to "leave the province" as soon as they could earn enough money to buy passage "to some part of the coast of *Africa*, where we propose a settlement." At the same time, other black New Englanders, both slave and free, were petitioning successive governors, hoping to induce the British crown to show sympathy to their cause. In 1774, African Americans in Massachusetts reminded Governor Thomas Gage, "We have in common with all other men a naturel right to our freedoms." They asked him to abolish slavery and to provide them with "some part of the unimproved land, belonging to the province, for a settlement."

In the Southern colonies, with enslavement more widespread and black literacy generally forbidden, the chances for a petition or public appeal remained slim—unless it came from an outspoken visitor. In the tumultuous spring of 1775, an African-born preacher named David visited Charleston. The young evangelist spoke to a private gathering of black and white Christians, and he refused to utter gentle pieties. Instead, David assured his audience that "God would send Deliverance to the Negroes, from the power of their Masters, as He freed the Children of Israel from Egyptian Bondage." White listeners suspected that "he meant to raise rebellion amongst the negroes," and David had to flee the town rapidly to avoid being hanged.

If enslaved Africans were finally to win deliverance in 1775, perhaps it would be with the aid of British forces. When shots were fired at Lexington in April, and later at Bunker Hill, blacks like Peter Salem joined the patriot forces, and eventually thousands more would follow during the course of the Revolutionary War. But many more, particularly in the South, saw the British as their likely ally, as court testimony reveals. In April, Thomas Jeremiah, a free black who worked as a pilot in Charleston harbor, took aside an enslaved dockworker named Sambo and told him, "There is a great war coming soon." He urged Sambo to "join the soldiers," because the impending war "was come to help the poor Negroes." Several months later, Jeremiah was accused of smuggling guns from a British warship to slaves in the Charleston vicinity. Fearful of black rebellion, patriot leaders in control of the town had Jeremiah publicly hanged and then burned as a brutal example to other African-American freedom fighters.

In other Southern colonies, black hopes for successful armed rebellion also ran high during 1775, and white fears of a slave uprising proved equally strong. In eastern North Carolina, rumors of revolt were widespread. When a plot was discovered in early July, the patriot Committees of Safety rounded up scores of African Americans, many of them armed. Suspected slaves were severely whipped in public, and some had their ears cut off. All those who spoke to their captors told a similar story. According to Colonel John Simpson, they said they were to rise up on the night of July 8, destroy the local community, and march toward the backcountry, where they expected to be met by armed British officials and "settled in a free government of their own." Blacks in Maryland had similar hopes of overthrowing their bondage. Their bold talk and actions infuriated the patriot leaders in Dorchester County, who finally moved to confiscate their weapons. In one day, they claimed to have taken up "about eighty guns, some bayonets, swords, etc."

As 1775 unfolded, black aspirations for freedom and English desires to frighten white radicals in America seemed to coincide. "Things are coming to that crisis," wrote British commander Thomas Gage in June, "that we must avail ourselves of every resource, even to raise the Negros, in our cause." This practical alliance emerged most dramatically in Virginia. The royal governor in Williamsburg, Lord Dunmore, had hinted in May his intention of "proclaiming all the Negroes free, who should join him." By autumn, the patriots had forced him to take refuge on a vessel from His Majesty's Navy, and Dunmore was sailing the coastline, encouraging black Virginians to escape to British ships. In November, he issued a proclamation emancipating any slaves who would join his forces, and black Virginians flocked to his banner. Within a month, he had more than 300 persons enrolled in his "Ethiopian Regiment," with the words "Liberty to Slaves" emblazoned across their uniforms.

Patriot leaders and Virginia planters expressed deep concern over the success of Dunmore's proclamation. Up and down the Chesapeake, and as far away as Georgia, enslaved blacks were making desperate efforts to elude their owners and come under the protective wing of the Royal Navy. On November 30, the *Virginia Gazette* spoke of "boatloads of slaves" struggling to reach British ships, but not all of them made it. For instance, two women and seven men "who had been endeavoring to get to Norfolk in an open boat" were apprehended before reaching their destination. When a contingent of blacks in Georgia gathered on Tybee Island near the mouth of the Savannah River, the local Committee of Safety secretly paid a band of Creek Indians to destroy them before they could reach British protection. Likewise, some of the South Carolina runaways who set up camp on Sullivan's Island near Charleston harbor were hunted down before they could board British ships.

Despite the high risk, hundreds of African Americans clamored safely aboard English vessels in the months after Lord Dunmore's proclamation. In late December 1775, George Washington expressed his fear of Dunmore's plan. The patriot commander wrote that if "that man is not crushed by spring, he will become the most formidable enemy America has; his strength will increase as a snow ball by rolling; and faster, if some expedient cannot be hit upon to convince the slaves and servants of the impotency of his designs." But during the spring of 1776, it was not General Washington who stopped the dramatic flow of black Virginians to join Lord Dunmore. Instead, an outbreak of smallpox in the crowded camps finally reduced the tide of hopeful refugees. Had it "not been for this horrid disorder," Dunmore wrote in June 1776, "I could have expected two thousand blacks; with whom I should have had no doubt of penetrating into the heart of this Colony." In the preceding months, however, hundreds of African Americans along the Atlantic Coast had jumped at the chance for freedom.

The dramatic story of Thomas Peters is typical. He had been born in Africa in 1738, among the Yoruba in what is now Nigeria. At age twenty-two, he was kidnapped by slave traders and deported to Louisiana aboard the French slave ship *Henri Quatre*. Unwilling to submit to enslavement in a strange land, he was whipped, branded, and shackled for repeated efforts to gain his freedom. By 1770, he had been sold to William Campbell, a Scotsman living in Wilmington, North Carolina, and a leading member of the Sons of Liberty. In the spring of 1776, when the British sloop *Cruizer* entered the Cape Fear River, Peters saw his chance. Along with a black friend named Murphy Steel, he escaped to the British and enlisted in a company of Black Pioneers made up of slaves from the Cape Fear region. Tom was later joined by his wife, Sally, and their daughter, Clairy, born in 1771. (Peters and Steel would go on to serve with the British during the Revolution, and after the war, Peters spent time in Canada and England, eventually migrating back to Africa with friends and family, shortly before his death in 1792.)

Scarcely three months after Thomas Peters left William Campbell, Thomas Jefferson drafted the Declaration of Independence. In the Revolutionary War that followed, numerous slaves took advantage of the continuing turmoil to seek their freedom, but most were disappointed. The new nation that was born out of the struggle over independence would fail to honor, in its Constitution, the stirring words of Jefferson's declaration that "all men are created equal." The vast majority of the country's half-million African Americans were still living in the South and still bearing the yoke of slavery in 1776. In the nineteenthth century, another strong-armed force would appear along the Atlantic seaboard that could prompt hundreds of expectant blacks to risk all. Once again, they would run away from their masters with the hope of receiving weapons and obtaining a chance to fight for their own freedom. But it would take more than three long generations before the expectations for freedom raised by the American Revolution could be met through the bloodshed of the Civil War.

Chronology

1526

Some of the Africans who accompanied Ayllón to the Carolina coast remain with Indians when Spanish depart.

1539

Black guide Esteban is killed by Zuni Indians after crossing the continent with Cabeza de Vaca.

1540

Gomez, one of the Spanish-speaking Africans with De Soto, remains in Carolina with *cacica* of Cofetachiqui.

1565

Africans help construct St. Augustine in Spanish Florida, the oldest non-Indian town in North America.

1586

Francis Drake frees Africans in the Spanish Caribbean but fails to make them part of England's colony at Roanoke.

1600

Isabel, daughter of a free Negro, is among blacks and mulattoes who join Oñate in colonizing New Mexico.

1612

Mulatto sailor Juan Rodriguez leaves a Dutch ship in the Hudson River to trade for furs among Indians.

1619

Dutch ship brings "twenty and odd" Africans to the English colony at Jamestown, in Virginia.

1644

For the first time, New England merchants send three ships to Africa to trade for gold dust and Negroes.

1662

Virginia statute declares that all children born in the colony are to inherit the status of the mother.

1663

England creates the Company of Royal Adventurers into Africa, replaced in 1672 by the Royal Africa Company.

1664

A Maryland law specifies that acceptance of Christian baptism has no effect upon the legal status of a slave.

1700

Slavery becomes legally sanctioned in the colonies of Pennsylvania and Rhode Island.

1708

Africans in South Carolina exceed Europeans, making it the only English mainland colony with a black majority.

1711

John Lawson and a black companion are killed by Indians in North Carolina at the start of the Tuscarora War.

1731

African-born Samba Bambara plans a slave revolt in French Louisiana and is executed with his co-conspirators.

1733

The Spanish king issues an edict granting freedom to any English slaves escaping to St. Augustine, Florida.

1739

An Angolan named Jemmy leads the Stono Rebellion in South Carolina, but efforts to reach Florida fail.

1741

A supposed slave plot in New York City leads to executions and charges of Spanish intervention.

1757

Quaker abolitionist John Woolman, one of the first Englishmen opposing slavery, travels through the South.

1765

Anti–Stamp Act demonstrations in Charleston lead to rumors of a slave plot and black calls for "Liberty!"

1770

Black sailor Crispus Attucks leads an attack on British soldiers and is killed in the Boston Massacre.

1772

Slavery is outlawed in England through the decision of Lord Mansfield in the Somerset Case.

1773

African-born Phillis Wheatley, age 19, publishes her book, *Poems on Various Subjects, Religious and Moral.*

1775

Virginia governor, Lord Dunmore, issues a proclamation offering freedom to slaves joining the British cause.

1776

Thomas Peters (a Yoruba living in North Carolina) and hundreds of other slaves join the British in hopes of gaining freedom.

Further Reading

GENERAL AFRICAN-AMERICAN HISTORY

Appiah, Kwame Anthony, and Henry Louis Gates, Jr. *Africana: The Encyclopedia of the African and African American Experience.* New York: Basic Civitas Books, 1999.

Blackburn, Robin. *The Making of New World Slavery: From the Baroque to the Modern, 1492–1800.* London: Verso, 1997.

Boles, John B. Black *Southerners, 1619–1869.* Lexington: University Press of Kentucky, 1983.

Foner, Philip S. *History of Black Americans: From Africa to the Emergence of the Cotton Kingdom.* Westport, Conn.: Greenwood, 1975.

Franklin, John Hope, and Alfred A. Moss, Jr. *From Slavery to Freedom: A History of African Americans.* 8th ed. New York: Knopf, 2000.

Giddings, Paula. *When and Where I Enter: The Impact of Black Women on Race and Sex in America.* New York: Bantam, 1985.

Harding, Vincent. *There Is a River: The Black Struggle for Freedom in America.* San Diego: Harcourt Brace, 1981.

Higginbotham, Evelyn Brooks, ed. *The Harvard Guide to African-American History.* Cambridge: Harvard University Press, 2001.

Hine, Darlene C., et al., eds. *Black Women in America.* Brooklyn, N.Y.: Carlson, 1993.

Johnson, Charles, and Patricia Smith. *Africans in America: America's Journey through Slavery.* New York: Harcourt, Brace, 1998.

Kelley, Robin D. G., and Earl Lewis, eds. *To Make Our World Anew: A History of African Americans*. New York: Oxford University Press, 2000.

Mintz, Sidney W., and Richard Price. *The Birth of African-American Culture: An Anthropological Perspective*. Boston: Beacon Press, 1992.

Piersen, William D. *From Africa to America: African American History from the Colonial Era to the Early Republic, 1526–1790*. New York: Twayne, 1996.

Quarles, Benjamin. *The Negro in the Making of America*. 3rd ed. New York: Macmillan, 1987.

Scott, William R., and William G. Shade, eds. *Upon These Shores: Themes in the African-American Experience*. New York: Routledge, 2000.

SLAVERY AND SLAVE CULTURE

Aptheker, Herbert. *American Negro Slave Revolts*. New York: Columbia University Press, 1943.

Berlin, Ira. *Many Thousands Gone: The First Two Centuries of Slavery in North America*. Cambridge: Harvard University Press, 1998

Bontemps, Alex. *The Punished Self: Surviving Slavery in the Colonial South*. Ithaca, N.Y.: Cornell University Press, 2001

Carney, Judith A. *Black Rice: The African Origins of Rice Cultivation in the Americas*. Cambridge: Harvard University Press, 2001.

Gomez, Michael A. *Exchanging Our Country Marks: The Transformation of African Identities in the Colonial and Antebellum South*. Chapel Hill: University of North Carolina Press, 1998.

Ferguson, Leland. *Uncommon Ground: Archaeology and Early African America, 1650–1800.* Washington: Smithsonian Institution Press, 1992.

Frey, Sylvia R., and Betty Wood. *Come Shouting to Zion: African American Protestantism in the American South and British Caribbean to 1830.* Chapel Hill: University of North Carolina Press, 1998.

Gomez, Michael A. *Exchanging Our Country Marks: The Transformation of African Identities in the Colonial and Antebellum South.* Chapel Hill: University of North Carolina Press, 1998.

Higginbotham, A. Leon, Jr. *In the Matter of Color: Race and the American Legal Process: The Colonial Period.* New York: Oxford University Press, 1978.

Holloway, Joseph E., ed. *Africanisms in American Culture.* Bloomington: Indiana University Press, 1990.

Jordan, Winthrop D. *White over Black: American Attitudes toward the Negro, 1550–1812.* Chapel Hill: University of North Carolina Press, 1968.

Kaplan, Sidney, and Emma Nogrady Kaplan. *The Black Presence in the Era of the American Revolution.* Rev. ed. Amherst: University of Massachusetts Press, 1989.

Kolchin, Peter. *American Slavery, 1619–1877.* New York: Hill & Wang, 1993.

Mullin, Michael. *Africa in America: Slave Acculturation and Resistance in the American South and the British Caribbean, 1736–1831.* Urbana: University of Illinois Press, 1992.

Raboteau, Albert J. *Slave Religion: The "Invisible Institution" in the Antebellum South.* New York: Oxford University Press, 1978.

Scherer, Lester B. *Slavery and the Churches in Early America, 1619–1819.* Grand Rapids, Mich.: William B. Eerdmans, 1975.

Smith, Billy G., and Richard Wojtowicz. *Blacks Who Stole Themselves: Advertisements for Runaways in the Pennsylvania Gazette, 1728–1790.* Philadelphia: University of Pennsylvania Press, 1989.

Stuckey, Sterling. *Slave Culture: Nationalist Theory and the Foundations of Black America.* New York: Oxford University Press, 1987.

REGIONAL STUDIES

Breen, T. H., and Stephen Innes. *"Myne Owne Ground": Race and Freedom on Virginia's Eastern Shore, 1640–1676.* New York: Oxford University Press, 1980.

Creel, Margaret Washington. *"A Peculiar People": Slave Religion and Community Culture Among the Gullahs.* New York: New York University Press, 1988.

Fischer, Kirsten. *Suspect Relations: Sex, Race, and Resistance in Colonial North Carolina.* Ithaca: Cornell University Press, 2002.

Hall, Gwendolyn Midlo. *Africans in Colonial Louisiana: The Development of Afro-Creole Culture in the Eighteenth Century.* Baton Rouge: Louisiana State University Press, 1992.

Hodges, Graham Russell. *Root and Branch: African Americans in New York and East Jersey, 1613–1863.* Chapel Hill: University of North Carolina Press, 1999.

Kay, Marvin L. Michael, and Lorin Lee Cary. *Slavery in North Carolina, 1748–1775.* Chapel Hill: University of North Carolina Press, 1995.

Landers, Jane. *Black Society in Spanish Florida.* Urbana: University of Illinois Press, 1999.

Littlefield, Daniel. *Rice and Slaves: Ethnicity and the Slave Trade in Colonial South Carolina.* Baton Rouge: Louisiana State University Press, 1981.

Morgan, Edmund S. *American Slavery, American Freedom: The Ordeal of Colonial Virginia.* New York: Norton, 1975.

Morgan, Philip D. *Slave Counterpoint: Black Culture in the Eighteenth-Century Chesapeake and Lowcountry.* Chapel Hill: University of North Carolina Press, 1998.

Olwell, Robert. *Masters, Slaves, and Subjects: The Culture of Power in the South Carolina Low Country, 1740–1790.* Ithaca: Cornell University Press, 1998.

Piersen, William D. *Black Yankees: The Development of an Afro-American Subculture in Eighteenth-Century New England.* Amherst: University of Massachusetts Press, 1988.

Sensbach, John F. *A Separate Canaan: The Making of an Afro-Moravian World in North Carolina, 1763–1840.* University of North Carolina Press, 1998.

Sobel, Mechal. *The World They Made Together: Black and White Values in Eighteenth-Century Virginia.* Princeton: Princeton University Press, 1987.

Tate, Thad W., Jr. *The Negro in Eighteenth-Century Williamsburg.* Charlottesville: University Press of Virginia, 1966.

Usner, Daniel H., Jr. *Indians, Settlers, and Slaves in a Frontier Exchange Economy: The Lower Mississippi Valley before 1783.* Chapel Hill: University of North Carolina Press, 1992.

Williams, William H. *Slavery and Freedom in Delaware, 1639–1865.* Wilmington: Scholarly Resources, 1996.

Wood, Betty. *Slavery in Colonial Georgia, 1730–1775.* Athens: University of Georgia Press, 1984.

Wood, Peter H. Black Majority: *Negroes in Colonial South Carolina from 1670 through the Stono Rebellion.* New York: Knopf, 1974.

BIOGRAPHIES AND WRITINGS

Carretta, Vincent, ed. *The Interesting Narrative and other Writings by Olaudah Equiano*. New York: Penguin, 1995.

Carretta, Vincent. "Olaudah Equiano or Gustavus Vassa? New Light on an Eighteenth-Century Question of Identity." *Slavery and Abolition*, Vol. 20, No. 3 (December 1999), 96–105.

Grant, Douglas. *The Fortunate Slave: An Illustration of African Slavery in the Early Eighteenth Century*. New York: Oxford University Press, 1968.

Richmond, Merle A. *Phillis Wheatley*. New York: Chelsea House, 1988.

Shields, John C., ed. *The Collected Works of Phillis Wheatley*. New York: Oxford University Press, 1988.

Yates, Elizabeth. *Amos Fortune, Free Man*. New York: Dutton, 1950.

Index

from West Africa, 31, 39–40,
41–46
See also Middle passage
Smith, John, 21
Smith, William, 65
Solomon, Job ben, 40–44, 70,
fig. 3
South Carolina
African-American population
in, 39
colonization of, 3
slave rebellion in, 78–79, 89, 91
Spanish colonies, 2–12, 25
Spanish explorers, 1–12
Stamp Act, 84–85, 87, 89
St. Augustine
British attack, 15
runaway refuge, 78, 81
settlement of, 8–10
Stedman, Cato, 87
Steel, Murphy, 94
Stone, James, 26–27

Stono Rebellion, 78–79
Sugarcane industry, 37, 50

Tar production, 51
Tobacco plantation, 42, 57
Tolsey, Alexander, 42
"Top dog," 49
Transportation systems, 50, 51

Verrazzano, Giovanni da, 8
Virginia colony, 15–16, 28, 33

Washington, George, 57–58, 93
Wheatley, Phillis, 67, 70, 89, fig. 7
Whitemore, Cuff, 87
Winthrop, John, 21
Women workers, 52–53
Woodworking, 49–50
Woolman, John, 88
Working conditions, 47–48

Zuni pueblo Indians, 5–6

Art Credits

Art Museum, Princeton University. Gift of Mrs. Gerald Wilkinson: cover; ©British Museum: fig. 4; Giraudon/Art Resource, New York: fig. 1; Library of Congress: frontispiece, fig. 5; Massachusetts Historical Society: fig. 7; Mortimer Rare Book Room, Smith College Library: fig. 3; from the collection of the New-York Historical Society: figs. 6, 8; New York Public Library, Print Collection, Astor, Lenox, and Tilden Foundation: fig. 2.

About the Author

PETER H. WOOD is a professor of history at Duke University. He holds a Ph.D from Harvard University and spent two years at Oxford University on a Rhodes scholarship. Dr. Wood is the author of *Black Majority: Negroes in Colonial South Carolina from 1670 through the Stono Rebellion*, which was nominated for the National Book Award. He is also the co-author of *Winslow Homer's Images of Blacks* and co-editor of *Powhatan's Mantle: Indians in the Colonial Southeast*. Wood is a lead author for the recent survey text, *Created Equal: A Social and Political History of the United States.*